Cl
AND
MADE
IN THE
FURNACE
OF
AFFLICTIONS

MW00629636

AUTHOR
RANATA M. BARRIER

PUBLISHED BY:

NU-VISIONS
INNOVATIONS, LLC

Unless otherwise noted, all Scripture quotations are
from King James Version of the Bible.

Scriptures noted AMP are taken from the Amplified
®Bible Copyright© 1954,1962, 1965, 1987 by the
Lockman Foundation. Used by permission.

Scripture quotations marked NIV are taken from the
Holy Bible, New International Version®, NIV®,
Copyright© 1973, 1978, 1984, 2011 by Biblica, Inc.™
Used by permission of Zondervan.

Scripture quotations marked NKJV are from the New
King James Version of the Bible. Copyright© 1979, 1980,
1982 by Thomas Nelson, Inc., publishers. Used by
permission.

Definitions taken from Merriam Collegiate Dictionary
Eleventh Edition, principal copyright 2003
Jacketed hardcover un-indexed: alkaline paper

Cover Design by **Otis Spears**

CHOSEN AND MADE IN THE FURNACE OF AFFLICTIONS
by Ranata M. Barrier

Published by Nu-Visions Innovations LLC
4960 Louisa Dr.
New Orleans, LA. 70126
Printed in the United States of America

Elder Ranata Barrier does a great job of articulating how our GOD, through the process of purification, refines us into His very image by the delicate controlled ministering of test, trials, and tribulation to perfect us for His Glory. It is clear through this literary work that GOD is the Potter and we are the clay and his quest is to bring about discipline over disorder and character over comfort that we may become who He has called us to be. Therefore, in the midst, of the fire we must always trust in GOD and understand the fact the flames are to develop us and not to devastate us. To GOD be the Glory.

Pastor Lionel Roberts, Sr.
Holy Anointed House of Prayer
New Orleans, LA.

As believers, we can know in our hearts that God is Sovereign and strong. We can believe that his plans for us are good and blessings are in store as we follow Him. Oftentimes, the greatest blessings come after the greatest times of trials and testing. God paved the way of freedom for Joseph. Even though it wasn't right away, slavery and imprisonment could not keep him contained. He will not waste your pain, but He will use the difficulties of your life to bring forth blessings, freedom, and promotion. I highly recommend the reading of this insightful book to give each reader discernment regarding God's purpose and calling for your life.

Prophetess Gail Pierce
Kingdom Life Ministries
Gretna, LA.

When we are overwhelmed through the pressures and transition of life, HE uses people as a vessel to intercede on our behalf to **RESTORE** or to have a **NEW** relationship with **HIM**. These are the times when we may ask "How did I get through this?"

GOD ALWAYS has the prefect plan. He prepares and send us through the "test" because He knows the end before the beginning. Again, when being tested and going through trials, your FAITH must manifest. I will call it the "Preparation Process." During our "test" and "preparation" our help will come from the LORD. Through our obedience and faith, He will bring us to NEW heights! But remember, the enemy will try to distract and destroy the people of GOD while they are on the path of blessings and restoration to keep them hopeless, oppressed, and depressed. But the people of GOD must remember to tap into their faith and know that their GOD will "never leave them nor forsake them!" Finally, during our afflictions we must wait upon the LORD and seek HIM.

Prophetess Beverly Lewis
Empowering for Life Prophetic Ministry
Marrero, LA.

The author brings such revelatory details about the "**Call**" and "**Choosing**" process. Her life experiences' shared, caused me, the reader, to begin to assess and think upon the numerous incidences of darkness, pain and trauma experienced in my personal life and now equate them to being precious blocks of times GOD set aside just to test, prove, transform, and re-create me because I have been **Called** and **Chosen**. My prayer is that every reader will receive this great revelation and

more, as they pursue through the papers of the awesome written work. Embrace, Stand in Awe, and Bless our GOD that you and I have been "**Chosen in the Furnace of Afflictions**".
Elder Treva Barrier Sanders

Chosen in the Furnace of Afflictions relates to all on the journey to a life, molded and shaped by the hands of the master. Whether you are seeking to know the will of the Father, in the process of a closer walk with the Father or a seasoned believer this book will minister to you.

Our lives are constantly being shaped as we find ourselves in several levels of the furnace. The initial firing, will make many cry, it is enough, saying they are content to sit right here on the pews. Just when you think, you are content, the Master gently picks you up again and ushers you into the furnace again.

Chosen in The Furnace of Afflictions, will encourage your heart to continue this wonderful journey by faith and trust in the hand of an all knowing, all loving Father. Allow your hearts to see, your furnace experiences with a positive outlook of hope, expectation, and deliverance.

Elder Ranata Barrier's open, transparency, and candor provides an understanding of the love, power, and wisdom of the Father. Her journey through each furnace of affliction, has produced strength and wisdom while opening a door to assist each of us. Transparency presents an opportunity of hope and strength enabling us to relate. Iron sharpens iron. Prepare your hearts to receive as you are **Chosen in the Furnace of Afflictions.**
Elder Seimorne Barton

CONTENTS

FOREWORD

𝔉ire, affliction and suffering are a part of a detailed Christian life! It's how we move from faith to faith and from glory to glory. How we rise from ashes to become the servants that God has commissioned in these last days.

I am proud to acknowledge Ranata Barrier as the tried and true candidate for this task of exposing the tactics of the enemy. She has captured the true essence of the struggle that saints encounter when living this life as a born-again kingdom citizen. Being closely related to each other due to brother and sister siblings, we also find ourselves related on each side of the cross.

Ranata addresses the issue of afflictions that present itself as a task for saints at each stage of his or her life. While we are confronted with these issues, the Scriptures and her testimony will be sure to help the seeker of God's face.

Spiritual warfare is an assignment that she has been given, which along with the anointing, to overcome and learn from every fiery furnace she has encountered. This book will help you with connecting with the reality of the fires that exist in your lives. It will allow you to get a better feel of the difference between what's fiction and fact.

When a personalized testimony is given to a reader, it's more than the speculation of others through statistics. When you hear the suffering of others and can relate in some ways, it opens the doors for healing to take place. The furnace that our God uses is not always cut and dry in understanding but is always effective. Transforming lives by giving the participants a personal testimony helps to bring about the reforming of others.

Pastor Alfred Balthazor
Mt. Beulah M.B. Church
Collins, Mississippi

DEDICATION

This book is dedicated to my two beautiful daughters, **Chaille White** and **Deryl (Dee) Nunnery**, for all the afflictions we've endured together. Those afflictions we experienced have made us stronger in the Lord and increased our faith in God and in each other. "Thank You" for helping me through some of the roughest times in my life and putting up with me when I knew it was unbearable at times. "Thank You" for sticking with me and allowing our relationship to heal. My prayer is that you will have enough knowledge and experience to handle the furnaces in your lives that would be pleasing unto God. You both are more than conquerors and you will come forth as pure gold. There is nothing too hard for God.

Now that you both are mothers, I pray that you will do your best to teach your children to be all that God has called them to be. "Thank You" for being so understanding of my call to help and mentor other young ladies. Yes, you had to share me with others, even when you did not want to. "Thank You" for giving me two of the most beautiful granddaughters, **Hailey Janay** and **Charlie Willow**. I love you both so much!!!

I also dedicate this book to my late **Aunt, Henrietta Carter (Auntie Yetta)**. At a young age she helped me through a lot of fires. Some fires I started, and some God created for me, to get me to the place He has destined for me. She always believed in me and the ministry God called me to. Her support, spiritually, physically, and financially, made it possible to endure my afflictions. She was always like a second mother to me. I am honored that she spent her last days upon this earth taking care of me while I was recovering from surgery; encouraging and sharing with me secrets of our family history. I love you and miss you dearly!

Lastly, I dedicate this book to every person who has gone through the fire, who may be in the fire now, or is coming out of the fire. You are CHOSEN and MADE IN THE FURNACE OF AFFLICTIONS.

I am a living testimony of God's deliverance and healing power.

With All My Love,
Ranata Barrier

ACKNOWLEDGMENTS

I want to thank **God**, my Savior, Healer, Deliverer, and most of all, my Refiner, for allowing me to go through the FURNACE. Lord You were faithfully right there with me in the midst, of the furnace. Thank You for delivering me through every fire while teaching me great lessons.

I am so grateful to my parents, **John** and **Xavier Barrier**, who has been the best examples life could offer. Truly, they have been in the fire for years. My father is a fighter against the odds and my mother is one of the best caregivers I have seen on this side of Heaven. I love you both so dearly and I realized without family I don't know where I would be. I thank you for encouraging me to become a business owner and for supporting me in the ministry God has called me to.

To my Sister, **Elder Treva Sanders**. Thank you for praying for me when I was lost and living an ungodly lifestyle. Thank you for countless hours you toiled and labored with me. I appreciate the endless hours of prayer and encouragement which poured from your heart. Your prayers were fervent and effectual. I know, all too well, of your furnace experiences you have been delivered from. I watched you endure the furnace of losing your son, but I also saw God standing with you and keeping you in the middle of it all. It truly is a blessing to work in ministry side-by-side with you - **"Sisters of Thunder"**.

To my Sister, **Dr. Kendra Barrier**. You have spent countless years in the fire battling health challenges and working long hours of school and your career. You pressed, persevered, and endured to do what you were called to do. Truly you were made in the furnace. You displayed great tenacity to finish your goal and keep your date with destiny.

Trea', you have encountered many fires as early as your teen years. There is greatness inside of you. God has so many things in store for you. He will not allow you to go through so much pain without blessing you with promises He has just for you. My prayer is that you walk by faith, and not by sight and remember, God has been good to you and He loves you so much.

Jordan, God has allowed you at a young age to go through a furnace experience. You have a special anointing on your life. As a little girl you said, you were going to be a business owner. There is a Leader inside of you. You remind me so much of me. I knew I was different. Don't let anyone shape or try to form your life but God. **Jordan**, you and **Trea'** are fighters and it is evident in both of your lives that God has great things in store for both of you.

To my nephew, **Melvin. <u>Gone, way too soon</u>**. You encountered some furnaces I don't know if I could handle. I know God had the last say in your life. Your last words penned, in the last days of your life gives me comfort to know your life was not in vain. You are in a better place. We all miss your laughter and sense of humor. **You may be gone, but never forgotten.**

To my nephew, **Christian**. You have also experienced many furnaces at your young age, they were not to harm you. The devil meant it for bad, but God is turning it for your good. I know you may not see right now, but God will reveal it to you in time. Losing a brother, father, and friend in a span of 3 years is not easy for a young man. Keep your focus and keep God first in your life. You are the only male figure left in our immediate family. The enemy wants to keep you from believing God is real. God is going to use you as a conduit for this family. These are big shoes to fill. Remember you can and will do all things through Christ who strengthens you. Keep pressing, don't quit, don't get distracted or detoured. There is no furnace too hot, no pressure too great, that you can't make it through. Victory is already yours. Walk in it.

To my Pastor and friend, **Prophetess Beverly Lewis**. I thank God for you. You pushed, prayed, and encouraged me when I felt like quitting. Years of counseling, prayer and molding helped me become a Woman of Divine Destiny. Every form of rebuke, correction and edification was not in vain. Truly you are a woman who has also suffered and gone through your many furnace experiences; but look at what God has and is doing in your life. You are a woman of small stature but operate in a powerful anointing. Every furnace you went through gave you a greater anointing to minister and deliver God's people. There is a Lion inside of you that should not be underestimated.

Pastor Lionel Roberts, I thank God for you. You heard God and believed in the calling God placed upon my life. Thank you for ordaining me to the office of an Elder and allowing me to serve in multiple areas of your ministry. Truly man of God, I have seen you go through your furnaces; yet God allowed you to stay humble and make it through. Now it is time for your promotion to step into the fullness of what God has for you.

Riva La Voy, I thank God for your trust in me, choosing me to assist in building a seven-month live-in transformation home for women who are being delivered from drugs, alcohol, domestic abuse, and homelessness. I learned how to war for the deliverance and healing of others through this program. I thank you for allowing me to help "**Rebuild lives one Miracle at a time.**"

I would like to thank **Elder Sheila Lister**, **Dr. Kendra Barrier** and **Elder Seimorne Barton** for spending time editing my book. I know the work you all put into it and I appreciate you all so much.

Thank you to every person who prayed for me, helped me, sowed into my life spiritually, emotionally, and financially. To every enemy which was used, I know it was part of the plan. I have been through the fire, but I don't look like what I've been through and I don't smell like fire or smoke. I survived because the fire inside me burned brighter than the fire around me. I have come to realize that I **AM CHOSEN**.

With Love and Appreciation!
Ranata Barrier

INTRODUCTION
"CHOSEN FOR THE FURNACE?"

"Behold, I have refined thee, but not with silver, I have chosen thee in the furnace of affliction" **(Isaiah 48:10)**

$\mathcal{T}$he **FURNACE** is a prepared place for all to experience. It does not exclude anyone. You can be a Christian, non-Christian, rich, poor, be a scholar or have no educational experience. It is designed for all races and religious backgrounds. It is inevitable that every created being will at some point in life experience a furnace through the means of trials, heartaches, sickness, disappointments, financial distress, or some situation which will affect their lives. Nothing or no one will stop this from happening. **"Why?"** you ask. Why must I endure hardships and yet don't know when they are to come? Will I have done something, said something, acted in a manner to cause the inevitable to enter my life? **Furnaces** are created due to either bringing the afflictions on ourselves because of sin, or disobedience. It is also created to bring a sinner to God, those in a backslidden state, or to refine the saints.

While some tests, ordeals, sufferings prove to be beneficial for the sake of the Gospel; we will come to the place where God has designed each of us to experience a furnace of afflictions. **The fire of the furnace is a fire of refinement designed to burn away impurities, sins,**

unwise choices; to cause us to be molded and shaped in the image of God's Son, Jesus Christ. We as believers should ponder the cause of our being placed in the furnace, but ultimately, pray for what the end shall be. Will I make it out? Will my life be changed for the betterment of God's kingdom? Will I be promoted to perform the task God has for me or what someone else has left undone? What will the end bring? Who goes into the furnace? Why and when does one go into the furnace?

These are the questions which arise when we think about the ordeal of someone having to be tried in the furnace.

> *Ye have not chosen me, but I have chosen you, and ordained you, that you should go and bring forth fruit, and that your fruit should remain"* **(John 15:16).**

> *"Behold, I have refined thee, but not with silver, I have chosen thee in the furnace of affliction"* **(Isaiah 48:10).**

Ecclesiastes 3:1 it states:
> *"To everything there is a season, and a time to every purpose under the heaven."*

In our Christian life there are various seasons we must endure. Each of the seasons has a purpose and each has five key factors: **(1) Character, (2) Faith, (3) Focus, (4) Warfare, and (5) Endurance.**

I.   CHARACTER

Some would ask the question, **"What is character?"** **Character is a** one of the attributes or features that make up and distinguish an individual. The season of going through the furnace has its purpose and is designed to test and build our character. Character is designed to bring forth fruit. Some synonyms of character are: complexion, disposition, make-up, or nature. The character we are to achieve is the Nature of God; to be made in God's image and likeness. Our character should look like and reflect the image of God. Your character determines when you will come out of the furnace.

To every Christian who is serious about their relationship with God. Those that want to know the God of the Bible; see signs, wonders and miracles, and want to walk in the anointing and in your purpose and destiny, **"you"** are the chosen one to go through the furnace of afflictions. I don't care what God has called and purposed you to do, if you hold a five-fold ministry office or not; if it is from Apostleship to Ministry of Helps, you will go through your own **furnace of afflictions**. There has been one specifically designed just for you, to make you a new person in the end; the person God ordained for you to be. You need to remember this, you must keep your **FOCUS** and know God is in control.

In **Jeremiah 29:11**, God said, *"For I know the thoughts that I think toward you, saith the LORD, thoughts of peace, and not of evil, to give you an expected end."*

God has already planned in His mind what He has prepared for us. The Bible says, *"that God knows the thoughts that He thinks towards us."* Notice, it did not say He spoke them into existence. We know from history once God spoke something into existence, it was so. But here God says, *"that He knows the thoughts that He has toward you, good and not evil."* However, there will be a furnace we will go through and endure to get to that expected end.

II. FAITH

Levels of faith are reached far beyond what your mind can comprehend. God says that, *"For my thoughts are not your thoughts, neither are your ways my ways"* **(Isaiah 55:8)**.

We do not know what the steps are to get us to our destination, but God always gives us a glimpse of the end. It is the process of getting to the end and things we will go through, that will cause us to take on the characteristics and the nature of God. It will be a faith walk all the way, because *"without faith it is impossible to please God"* **(Heb. 11:6)**. Our faith will be tested and tried to levels which we would have not been able to understand if He would have shown it to us. God takes us on a journey that we would never comprehend. We will experience things that we would not have imagined we would have to deal.

III. FOCUS

Focus is another key factor in making it through the furnace. There are things that the enemy will specifically design to make you lose your focus and get you sidetracked. It is in those times God promises His chosen, who constantly seek Him, to help them stay on the right path. **Psalm 32:8** says, *"I will instruct thee and teach thee in the way which thou shalt go: I will guide thee with mine eye."*

IV. WARFARE

Levels of warfare will take place while going through your furnace experience. You must literally fight to stand on the promise of the Word. You must proclaim what the Word of the Lord says concerning your life. You must fight! You are in the army of the Lord. <u>There will be times of pulling down strongholds, casting down imaginations, binding and loosing, speaking "It is written," taking a stand, crying out to God, encouraging yourself in the Lord, laying prostrate on your face and praying in the Spirit.</u> At times you may not even be able to pray or read your Bible with comprehension. But God is faithful, He will send the right person with a prayer, Scripture, song, a television program, the right sermon, or just a plain ordinary sign. He will encourage you, lift you, and get you back on track.

V. ENDURANCE

Endurance is the last major factor in the process of your furnace of afflictions experience. It will determine your outcome. The Bible says in **Ecclesiastes 9:11,** *"I returned, and saw under the sun,* *that the race is not to the swift, nor the battle to the strong, neither yet bread to the wise, nor yet riches to men of understanding, nor yet favour to men of skill; but time and chance happeneth to them all."* Many quote, "the race is not given to the swift, nor the battle to the strong, but to him that endure to the end." **Matthew 24:13,** *"But he that shall endure unto the end, the same shall be saved."*

It does not matter how fast you go through your furnace experience, or how strong or weak you may be in the midst. The key is to endure through it all and not to give up or give in.

Various types of test and trials are specifically designed and prepared for you individually. My test and trial will not be like anyone else's. There may be some similarities, but the exact outcome and plan will never be the same. Obstacles are opportunities for you to overcome. They help you grow stronger and receive more revelation of who God really is once the obstacles are accomplished. We will not know God as a deliverer or healer until He reveals this in your life. **Psalm 34:19** says, *"Many are the afflictions of the righteous: but the Lord delivereth him out* *of them all."* The many afflictions you will encounter the Lord will deliver you from every one of them, however, you must be tried in the fire to come out as pure gold.

The enemy will try to make you compromise your values. At times the pain will become so great, you may suffer in untold manners. The enemy will also try to bring you gifts, or solutions that would seem to ease your pain. This is to get you to move ahead of God or come out of the fire before it is your time.

Our Father will allow these times of testing to see if you will be weak enough to fall for the things that look like a blessing instead of the **"real deal"**. Just wait for the promise. God's grace is sufficient to see you through.

> **I Peter 5:10** says, *"But the God of all grace, who hath called us unto His eternal glory by Christ Jesus, after that ye have suffered a while, make you perfect, stablish, strengthen, settle you."*

Why don't you just surrender today and allow the Lord to make the vessel He created and purposed? It is the beginning of an experience you will never forget; one of transformation and destination. God has prepared the furnace for you so that you can come forth as pure gold. He is molding and shaping you to be a vessel of Honor that He has called you to be. He will make you that signet ring He desires to use so that others will know that you have been **CHOSEN!**

ANSWER THE CALL

Who knew my final fellowship with my friend Carolyn would turn into something so serious? I had no idea there had been a call placed on my life. The circumstances to follow would only be the beginning of a setup by God for the place He would bring me to; a place in Him. I could not see at the time that there are no coincidences in life. Everything we go through has been orchestrated by the conductor Himself, God our Father.

One Friday afternoon in December of 1987, my best friend Carolyn, and I were sitting at my kitchen table reflecting on the last three years of our lives while drinking our daiquiris (I had not accepted the Lord into my life yet and still was a drinker). Carolyn, a very kind and gentle person had been my roommate, friend, and co-worker during the time I resided in Atlanta, Georgia. At times, we had serious disagreements, differences, and disasters! We shared much because we had been through many serious times together. There were things we thought we would not get through, but we did. She assisted me for years with raising my girls (I was a single parent of two) and she was my adopted family in Atlanta.

For some reason, (one God-ordained reason), this day was different, and Carolyn was insisting on reflecting on the past. She talked about the good times and the bad times. We cried and laughed together and yet she seemed to be consumed with our past on this night.

We had been friends for seven years and had finally come to a level of maturity, we lacked in the earlier years. She said she knew we had changed and she was glad our friendship weathered all the storms. She expressed to me she never had a friend like me before and was glad God brought me into her life. At this point in my life, I don't remember talking much about God. I knew of God, I was raised in a Catholic home, attended Catholic school, went to church every Sunday, but I had not accepted God into my life. I really didn't know Him. I was living a life of worldliness and was blinded to the things of God.

I listened as she continued her journey of the past. Sharing stories of how she went to the doctor for years before she was diagnosed with Systemic Lupus Erythematosus (SLE). This brought back memories of how I read all kinds of articles and materials on lupus to aid her with understanding her illness. I remembered her terrible bouts with lupus, and the effects it had on her life, her body, and how it even played a part in her death. She began telling of her current situation of how the

Pharmacist filled all her prescription bottles with the same medication. At the time, she was taking prednisone (a steroid) and plaquenil (an immune-suppressant). The pharmacist mistakenly filled both bottles with plaquenil.

Carolyn had just gone to the doctor and received a good progress report. She also received a prescription, decreasing the dosage of her prednisone. Five days had gone by before she realized her medication was incorrect. Carolyn said she was feeling extremely tired. As she was sitting at the table one morning she noticed all her medication was the same. As she reached for the bottles, she examined her medication, and realized, five days later, the mistake made. She had no prednisone. She returned to the doctor only to find out she had blood clots all over her body. To correct the error made by the pharmacist, the doctor ordered an increase in her prednisone to bring her disease under control. Carolyn even expressed concern of possibly suing the pharmacists for such an irresponsible mistake. As I look back, I had no idea I would have to deal with the same dreaded disease with my own daughter.

For some odd reason, she continued reminiscing about her past, speaking about how most of all bad situations work out for the good. Except, for an incident with her mother and aunt (her mother's sister) which bothered her so much it caused her pain. She began to cry while telling of her grandmother's passing away a few years ago, and how her mother and aunt had been feuding.

They had not spoken to each other for years, over the property left by her grandmother. She said they had not spoken to each other in years and this really bothered her because she knew her mother was very lonely and needed her sister. Carolyn's mother and aunt were Christian women who served God and were active in their local churches, but were not ready to stop allowing the enemy to divide them. Through her tears, she said she "would do anything to see the two of them together again" because they were once so very close. Who knew Carolyn's exact words were *the beginning of a life change for me.*

We reminisced for hours that night, I invited her to spend the night since it had gotten very late, and I knew she did not have any transportation. She insisted she needed to go home even though it was late. I was unable to bring her home because we had too many drinks. The streets of Atlanta were much too dark at night to be driving under the influence. She picked up the telephone and called a cab. As she was leaving she turned around, gave me a big hug, told me how much she loved me, and expressed once again she was glad I was her friend. I had no idea at that moment it would be the last time I would see Carolyn. This night was *the beginning of a change for me.*

The next day, the conversations we held the night before were imprinted so clearly in my mind. There was something very different about what had taken place. Something so unexplainable. Later that day, I received a call from Carolyn's boyfriend asking me what Carolyn had to eat and drink at my house on the previous night. He said she became gravely ill, was rushed to the hospital, and the doctor was seeking any information he could to aid him in diagnosing her condition. I remember trying to contact her during the day, but I was unable to because she had a series of tests scheduled.

The next day Carolyn was so heavy on my mind. This day was different from all the other days she was in the hospital. There was something so pressing on me, that I needed to share with her. When I finally spoke with her, she sounded as if she had no voice. She said she could not really talk to me and felt bad because she could not do so. Carolyn wanted me to know how much she loved me. That was my final time ever hearing her voice and her telling me she loved me. Those final words would ring in my ears for the rest of my life.

The next day I received the most devastating call which would affect my life forever. I was told Carolyn did not make it. Immediately, all kinds of thoughts began to flood my mind. I was devastated, hurt, angry and saddened. I became hysterical and did not know what to do. I wondered if my allowing her to drink could have caused her condition to worsen. Why did she have all those conversations with me about the past? Did she know this was going to happen? Why did she leave me like this? I was not prepared for this. I had never experienced anything like this before and I did not know what to do. My mind could not stop racing. I had a million questions and I had no one to ask. All I knew was a major person in my life, my only family in Atlanta, was taken away from me and I didn't know what to do. I began to cry out for help. I did not have anyone to talk to about this situation. The only person I knew to call was my mother. I remember being in a state of confusion and not being able to function, but I remember my mother consoling me over the telephone.

It is really calming when a mother can minister to her child to give her peace in a time of turmoil. She just seemed to have a way to make it all better. She genuinely cared and consoled me the best way she knew how.

I managed to pull myself together long enough to travel 75 miles to Columbus, Georgia, which was Carolyn's hometown. A caravan of people made the trip to the funeral. Imagine a 75-mile trip with hardly any discussion and complete uneasiness. None of us knew what to expect, and none of us, especially me, was prepared for such an event. We buried Carolyn five days before Christmas. What a trying time. I had sent the girls home to New Orleans to spend time with their grandparents knowing it would be a difficult time for all of us. I wanted my girls to have a pleasant holiday. Things that were happening in my life that I could not even begin to explain.

I remember sitting in the church feeling numb, thinking to myself, this was not real. I felt like I was dreaming. It seemed as if the services lasted forever. I remember as I was leaving the funeral, Carolyn's mother was standing in the back of the church. I walked up to her and gave her a big hug. She turned to her side and said she wanted to introduce me to her sister. Immediately my mind was redirected to the last time Carolyn and I were together. Carolyn had told me she would give anything to see her mother and her aunt together again. I could not understand why this was happening after she was gone. Didn't Carolyn deserve the chance to see her mother and aunt together?

I began to ponder this while at the gravesite. Later we went to Carolyn's mother's house after the funeral. We ate, fellowshipped, and talked about Carolyn.

I finally had a moment alone with Carolyn's mother. I shared with her how happy I was to see her and her sister together and how I knew Carolyn would have been so happy to see this reunion, but for a happier occasion. Carolyn's mother began to cry after hearing Carolyn's desire and she ushered me into her bedroom. She proceeded to tell me something that would shake me up to the point that I would never be the same again.

Carolyn's mother, who was a born-again Christian for years, told me she understood why I had to tell her about Carolyn's desire. It helped shed some light on why all of this happened. She shared the events of her day the Saturday before Carolyn died. She was outside washing her car when the Holy Spirit instructed her to go inside, call her sister and have a conversation with her. Carolyn's mother said she refused at first. The voice of the Holy Spirit came again, stronger, and told her to go inside and call her sister. The Holy Spirit instructed Carolyn's mother to tell her sister she was forgiven. Carolyn's mother said she could not deny the presence of the Holy Spirit and, in obedience, retreated into her house. She did not hesitate because the unction of the Holy Spirit was very strong. She called her sister, whom she had not spoken to in years, and told her she forgave her and wanted to know how she was doing. Carolyn's mother said their conversation was very brief, but a very good one. She then returned outside to finish washing her car.

Her mother said she began to feel such a peace fall upon her which was indescribable as she felt a weight being lifted from her. As this inner peace was happening, she had no idea Carolyn was sick or even in the hospital. Late Sunday night, Carolyn took a turn for the worst. The doctor called Carolyn's sister and told her to get the immediate family to the hospital as soon as possible. Carolyn's sister knowing the distance of the drive (75 miles), did not want her mother driving by herself while dealing with the severity of the situation; especially since she had no idea of what was going on with Carolyn. She decided to call her aunt asking her to bring their mother to Atlanta. Carolyn's sister knew her mother and aunt had not spoken for years, but she had no one else to call. She was unaware of the amends made the day before. The aunt agreed, picked up Carolyn's mother and headed to the hospital in Atlanta to see Carolyn. Carolyn's mother said it was not until she and her sister were on the way to Atlanta when the Holy Spirit spoke to her telling her to look at what was taking place. This was one of the reasons Carolyn's mother was urged to call her sister because the Holy Spirit knew she would need her sister at that time. She continued telling me she and her sister entered Carolyn's hospital room in the wee hours of the morning. When Carolyn saw the two of them walk into the hospital room together she smiled at them and then she died. She lived long enough to see her specific desire happen before she died. Carolyn became the sacrifice for healing and restoration in her family.

As Carolyn's mother sat there with tears in her eyes sharing this most unbelievable story with me, a fear gripped me that I had never felt before. At that instance, something happened to me. Something so unexplainable yet, so serious. I remember a chill went across my body and an urgency to run to my home and lock myself in my room. Everything had changed. The explanation of this story told me that something took place that not even I could deny. I saw the hand of God in this situation, a God I knew about, but had not personally gotten to know and learn His ways. A God that I heard about but never took Him seriously until that very moment. It was at this point in my life that I knew I could not turn and go back to the way I was. I could no longer deny that God existed and that the power of God was great!

I returned to Atlanta that night and locked myself in my room only to cry out to God and ask Him why and what exactly was happening? I could not understand why I was feeling the way I was feeling. There was not anyone to call because all my friends were in the world and they would not understand what I was going through.

I could not even understand what was happening to me and I knew I could not give an explanation they would understand. I sensed a major change was taking place in my life, but I had no idea what it was. I locked myself in my bedroom for approximately two weeks. As strange as it may seem, I remember receiving a telephone call during that two-week period. That call had a profound meaning. It was from a friend who later became my husband. He began to share the Word of God and ministered to me. I thank God for the telephone call because it helped me in a tremendous way. Even though I did not know God, he heard my cry and sent someone to minister to me.

I remember in high school we would tease each other and kid around because he and his family were always in church. At the time, I never really understood how anyone spent so much time in church. He and his family traveled all over the world singing with groups and choirs. Now the same person I teased was the same person God sent to minister to me in the time of need. His ministering flowed so easily. I am not sure if it was because he had the pleasure of meeting Carolyn the year before when she spent holidays with me and my family in New Orleans.

Not much transpired between us except that God allowed him to minister to me when I was in distress. I could no longer function as the person that I had been. Everything had changed, and I was beginning to feel uncomfortable in the environment I was currently living in. My lifestyle had to change. I had no clear understanding of the first steps to take. I began to search and seek out what I was supposed to be. The life of drugs, alcohol, and worldly living had to come to a halt. I felt compelled to move. I knew I needed to change my atmosphere and my life. Therefore, my journey began. I moved from Atlanta to Houston.

I stayed in Houston only three months. It did not work out well for me. I was looking for help in all the wrong places. I moved my girls twice in a matter of four months to two different states. When you are sensing that change must come, there will be times when you don't know how to seek God for the answers. I knew I was searching to find my place, and purpose, but had no idea of which way to go or what was happening in my life. I moved back to New Orleans after living in Atlanta for seven years (God's number of completion). The job I had in Atlanta was with a large construction company which was black-owned. The company transferred me from the Department of Energy in New Orleans to their job site in Atlanta when I was only 21 years old. I did not realize that it was the favor of God on my life at such a young age. I was given great experiences and opportunities. God was ordering my steps, even though I was not serving Him at this point in my life.

Now, back in New Orleans, I was a different person than when I left. I started working in a beauty salon. I sensed God was calling me out of my worldly ways. I began to feel and know that my lifestyle was not pleasing to God. I got baptized, committed myself to consistent Bible study and Sunday school, as I continued to work in beauty salons in New Orleans.

I found myself moving from one beauty salon to another searching for an environment where my Christian faith could grow and where God could use me. I had not learned what it was to be a beacon of light, but the struggle continued as I found myself in places that easily compromised my walk. I was determined to change and not succumb to the lifestyle of working with others who encouraged me to get high and live on a roller coaster ride.

For eight years (number of new beginnings), I worked in salons until God allowed me to shift to a new realm. I began working for one of my clients who owned a Home Health business.

When I transitioned to my new job, my sister-in-law invited me to my first prophetic meeting; held in a beauty salon. I had never been in a service that was held by a prophet before. This prophet spoke of Joseph going from the pit to the palace. The prophet called me to the altar. I had not been prophesied to before, so I was scared. In my mind, I said, "Don't let him touch me."

As I approached, he said, "I am not going to touch you or lay hands on you." I thought to myself, "He must have read my mind." He began to prophesy how my life was like Joseph and God was going to allow me to be become a business woman and to own and manage multiple businesses. He said I would go through hardships, yet I would have much favor on my life and God would be with me through it all. He said I would go from the pit to the palace. That night was approximately 25 years ago. How vividly I remember it!

It took a big step leaving my current position to begin working for someone else. God had a bigger plan. Little did I know, I would find favor on this job which would also be helpful for the furnace I was about to step into. Working in beauty salons, I had no benefits, no insurance or financial security. The new job, provided health insurance, an awesome salary, and a 9 to 5 schedule; I had more time to spend with my teenage daughters. What a difference, no more late nights, or all day on Saturdays. Better hours, more time at home and and much favor on the new job. I began to work with two Christian Certified Public Accountants (CPA) who favored me and began teaching me the intricate operations of the financial office. The health insurance coverage was a blessing. My daughter started having non-specific symptoms and eventually was diagnosed with lupus. It is imperative to allow God to order your footsteps. He has a plan and He is the only one who can orchestrate when and where the right time and place is for you. His timing is everything. There were people in my life who could not understand why I would stop working for myself to work for someone else. God had a plan.

Being in a new environment, made me hungry and thirsty for God and ready for this NEW change. I was ready for the transition. I knew I had to answer the call. It wasn't just a call of salvation, but a realization of having a call on my life to minister. I said, "Yes, God. I will go where You tell me to go. I will do what You have called me to do. I will say what You want me to say. Yes, I will be what You have predestined me to be." ***Yes, I answered the call!***

Chapter Two

CALLED AND CHOSEN

"Ye have not chosen me, but I have chosen you, and ordained you, that ye should go and bring forth fruit, and that your fruit should remain: that whatsoever ye shall ask of the Father in my name, he may give it you" **(John 15:16)**

CALLED

Webster's definition of **"CALLED"** - To be invited to come; to command to meet me; a holy calling from upon high.

Many are invited, but not all are chosen. Many will not withstand the pressures and adversity it takes to be chosen. Jesus used this phrase after He spoke a parable in which someone was invited to a wedding and did not have on a wedding garment. In the parable, Jesus likened the call to a King who had a marriage banquet for his son and those who were called/invited to the wedding, but, they would not come. The King sends his servants once again to tell them that the dinner was prepared, and all things were ready, but they didn't heed, some ignored and continued to go on with their lives. The King then compels His servants to go into the highway and as many as they find, bid them to come to the marriage banquet, and many came both good and bad. Notice when the invited were gathered all were not perfect but they heard the invitation and responded. The key is to respond to the invitation, to answer His bidding, and be included in the "few". *"For many are called, but few are chosen"* **Matt 22:14**.

> **II Timothy 1**:9: *"Who hath saved us, and called us with a holy calling, not according to our works, but according to his own purpose and grace, which was given us in Christ Jesus before the world began."*

CHOSEN

Webster's definition of *"CHOSEN"* - To be selected freely and after consideration; to have a preference for; one who is the object of choice or divine favor; an elect person.

> **Deuteronomy 7:6**, *"For thou art an holy people unto the LORD thy God: the LORD thy God hath chosen thee to be a special people unto himself, above all people that are upon the face of the earth."*

There are three types of people reading this book:

1.) Those who are "**in**" the furnace right now

2.) Those who "**will be going through**" the furnace soon

3.) Those who are "**coming out**" of the furnace now

Who is chosen and what are they chosen to do?

> **I Corinthians 1:26-27**, *"For ye see your calling, brethren, how that not many wise men after the flesh, not many mighty, not many noble, are called: But God hath chosen the foolish things of the world to confound the wise; and God hath chosen the weak things of the world to confound the things which are mighty."*

> **John 6:44**, (NIV) *"No one can come to me unless the Father who sent me draws Him. And I will raise him up on the last day."*

In this Scripture, Jesus is clarifying that no one can come on their own but is drawn by the Holy Spirit. The Greek word for "come" is "erchomai" meaning "to come from one place to another." Therefore, no one can come to Christ unless the Father draws them. The Greek word for "draw" is "helko" meaning to "drag" or to "draw" by an inward power. Even though God is the one who calls and has pre-destined us before the foundations of the world we have a responsibility to respond and be drawn by the inward power, the Holy Spirit.

Isaiah 41:8-9, *"But then, Israel art my servant, Jacob whom I have chosen, the seed of Abraham, my friend. Thou whom I have taken from the ends of the earth, and called thee from the chief men thereof, and said unto thee, Thou, art my servant: I have chosen thee, and not cast thee away."*

It is the person least expected, who is the one **Chosen,** the drug dealer, the gambler, the thief, the drug user, the prostitute, the troublemaker, the single parent and even those who once worked in corporate America and are now being called out to preach and evangelize. God's desire is for every one of them to come from one place to another and share the good news (Gospel.) I can see how God was calling me away from the world, a nobody to a new place in Him.

As we see in the above Scripture **(Isaiah 41:8-9)**, God chose Jacob, "the trickster", "the surplanter", before he was transformed, and was given a new identity and a new name. Jacob had to wrestle with the angel of God before his transformation manifested. This shows that God has no respect of persons.

As the Scriptures began to germinate, cultivate, and activate, I came to realize that I was **called** and **chosen.** I wanted fruit that would remain. The Scripture says that our fruit will remain **(John 15:16).**

Webster defines *"REMAIN"* as – **(1)** continue to exist, especially after other similar or related people or things have ceased to exist; **(2)** stay in the place that one has been occupying; **(3)** continue to possess a particular quality or fulfill a designated role.

Our fruit should remain, stay consistent, not wavering, not be double-minded, but stand firm on the Word of God and all His promises. In this Bible passage, Jesus was speaking directly to His disciples. Some questioned and wanted to know how or why these disciples were chosen. In their eyes, that person did not meet the qualifications, standard and lifestyle, yet, they were the chosen ones. So, do not let anything prevent you from being God's choice.

God needs His chosen ones to minister, preach and teach the Word of God, to lay hands on the sick, to release those imprisoned in their mind and entangled in bondage. By the work of the Holy Spirit we are called to bear His fruit. **(Galations 5:22).** *"For the tree is known by its' fruit, so will you be known by the fruit you bear."*

The Spirit reveals truth, guides, directs, convicts, and restrains. His *"fruit is love, joy, peace, longsuffering, gentleness, goodness, faith, meekness, and temperance"* **(Galations 5:22-23)**.

The Word also says God ordained you and has given you authority to do what He called you to do.

Webster defines *"ORDAIN"* - To invest with ministerial or priestly authority; to confer holy orders upon; prearrange unalterably.

If God **called** and **chose** you, He has placed a holy order upon your life. In accordance with the definition, "He prearranged His investment and cannot be altered." You have been predestined and ordained to bring forth fruit; the kind of fruit that will remain. As a seed falls to the ground and dies, to become something else, the seed must transform and transfigure into another being before it bears fruit. The process of becoming something else is much more than we can handle. We know we cannot do this on our own, we must rely on the perfect work of the Holy Spirit.

> **Roman 8:28-30** says, *"And we know that all things work together for good to them that love God, to them who are the called according to his purpose. For whom he did foreknow, he also did predestinate to be conformed to the image of his Son, that he might be the firstborn among many brethren. Moreover, whom he did predestinate, them he also called: and whom he called, them he also justified: and whom he justified, them he also glorified."*

God works all things out for your good, but only for those who are "**called according to his purpose**" and not according to **our** purpose. This verse tells us, we did not choose Him, but we participate in the call. **God chose us and those He chooses, He calls.**

> **John 15:1-5** states, *"I am the true vine, and my Father is the husbandman. Every branch in me that beareth not fruit he taketh away: and every branch that beareth fruit, he purgeth it, that it may bring forth more fruit. Now ye are clean through the word which I have spoken unto you. Abide in me, and I in you. As the branch cannot bear fruit of itself, except it abide in the vine; no more can ye, except ye abide in me. I am the vine, ye are the branches: He that abideth in me, and I in him, the same bringeth forth much fruit: for without me ye can do nothing."*

The evidence of fruit comes when you stay connected to the vine. You must be yielded and controlled by the Spirit of God, so your life can produce evidence of the Spirit. When you are attached to the vine you cannot detach or move away to do what you want to do. When you are attached to the vine, your steps are divinely, ordered by God. This means you cannot say what you want to say, your words must reflect what Jesus would say. When you are attached to the vine you should speak and seek progression and not regression.

> **John 15:7** says, *"If you abide in me and my words abide in you, ye shall ask what ye will and it shall be done unto you."*

Webster defines *"ABIDE"* as - to remain in place, to be sure or firm; endure.

The **Called** and **Chosen** must remain firm and fixed in the Lord as they faithfully endure through both good and bad times. **Psalm 37:23a**, *"The steps of a good man are ordered by the Lord."* **GOD EVEN ORDERS YOUR STEPS INTO THE FURNACE**; going through bad times are not always from the devil.

> **Isaiah 48:10** says, "He has chosen you in the furnace of affliction."

Look at it as being similarly to making gold; it will go through the fire. All the impurities and dross must be removed. When it is fully done, the goldsmith can see his image in the liquid gold. This is the same process the Lord is doing with us in the furnace. When He finishes refining us with fire we will look just like Him. We will become a church without spot or blemish.

Do not complain when going through trials and tribulations, God is getting the impurities out. As God is killing your flesh through continuous trials, remember to ask Him what He is showing or teaching you through the experience.

What fruit are you producing while going through this fiery trial? Keep focused on what you are going through and not focused on the lives of others. Don't point out what someone is going through but recognize the fire of God's purification. It is another part of the flesh being crucified, purged, and cleansed. As mentioned before, being placed in the furnace kills the works of the flesh leading to bearing the fruit of the Spirit. The Scripture states being ordained to bear fruit means the fruit will remain.

> **2 Timothy 2:19-21** says, *"Nevertheless the foundation of God standeth sure, having this seal, The Lord knoweth them that are his. And, let everyone that nameth the name of Christ depart from iniquity. But in a great house there are not only vessels of gold and of silver, but also of wood and of earth; and some to honour, and some to dishonour. If a man therefore purge himself from these, he shall be a vessel unto honour, sanctified, and meet for the master's use, and prepared unto every good work."*

In our process, we find it difficult to deal with the changes we endure. We may say, "Lord, this is too difficult to bear. Why do I have to change? This is uncomfortable." No one wants to go through anything that is hard or painful, but this is God's way of changing you. **CHANGE IS NOT CHANGE UNTIL IT IS CHANGED. IF IT IS GOING TO CHANGE, SOMETHING MUST BE CHANGED.** In your process, stop expecting or waiting on others to change, let the change begin in you. Therefore, you cannot continue doing what you have always been doing and expect a change. Your thought pattern, perception, and vision must change. Begin to look at situations differently and confess what the Word says about the situation. Remember, when going through your furnace experience, God is not changing your brother or sister, God is changing "you."

The Lord will use your sisters and brothers as cleansing and purifying agents, and He will constantly question you. He wants to know:

1) Are you going to do what you are supposed to do even when others are not?
2) Will you speak to others even if others do not speak to you?
3) Will you do what I called you to do even if others speak bad of you and spread rumors about you?
4) Will you listen to what others are going through even if you are going through yourself?
5) Will you do what I called you to do even if others do not understand?
6) Can you love your enemy?
7) Can you do good to those that use you?
8) Can you really bless others even when they curse you?
9) Can you really forgive others that have wronged you and said ugly things about you?
10) Can you turn the other cheek?

11) Can you trust Me even when you are unable to trace Me?
12) Can you speak those things that be not as though they were?

I went through a divorce after 12 years of marriage. I believed God was going to heal my marriage. I prayed and fasted for years believing that because my husband and I were both in ministry, that would be the prerequisite for healing our marriage. At the time, he was a praise and worship leader and I was a minister. I thought the thing we were going through was only a test. I never believed my spouse would leave and my marriage would dissolve after 12 years.

Divorce is like going through death, the loss of a loved one, especially when you have been connected to a person spiritually and emotionally for a long period of time. Through the years of interaction, soul-ties are developed. I remember going through bouts of depression after my divorce. It was as though I had lost a part of myself. I literally had to fight to keep my thoughts and right frame of mind. I was tormented and embarrassed for not being able to make this marriage work, even with both of us serving God. There were times I lost my focus while fighting to keep it together. This was a real boxing match. I had to fight in court for what was rightfully mine. I fought to have a stable home for my girls but eventually was forced to settle the property by selling the house and moving.

This was a hard blow, but after spending time in bed for some weeks, the Lord asked, "Are you still going to serve Me even if I did not heal your marriage?" The question hit me with a hard blow, but it caused me to come to my senses. Was I going to quit serving God because my marriage did not work or was I going to heed the Call placed upon my life? As I pondered in my heart, I knew God was calling me to yet another level. With unbearable pain, I felt rejected and often emotionally abused. I remember getting up at 2 a.m. and 3 a.m. to pray in the spirit. It was in those times, that my Heavenly Father was preparing me for the next furnace.

I remember lying in the bed crying out to God because I was hurting. He responded with, "I am trying to set you free." I often questioned God asking Him what was wrong with me? What did I do to deserve this? Was allowing my heart to be broken a part of the plan? How could this happen when both of us were serving the Lord? There were people in the church who did not even know we were married. My husband had a way of appearing to be single. I aided in the appearance also, because we rarely participated in church or other events as a family, even if we were going to the same place. We drove separate cars because his car was not big enough for the family or he had to be there extremely early.

There were several challenges in the marriage. He desperately wanted a son, but because of health issues I was unable to have any more children. He was fully aware of this fact before we married, however, it was a greater strain on the marriage towards the end; leaving me feeling inadequate and barren. We had three girls between us and he rarely provided any parenting support because his music kept him busy and away from home, therefore, causing me to raise the girls by myself. I was married but living as a single person and a single parent. Anytime there was a step forward, there were three steps backwards. He would come home in the wee hours of the morning, leaving no time for us which desperately strained our communication. Two years we lived apart in the same house. The girls often stated how embarrassed they were of our living situation. The signs of deterioration were there, but I kept praying, believing God to heal and restore.

There were rumors of infidelity, without any concrete evidence until the last year we were together. He became careless, leaving small signs. Even with the evidence, I still believed we could work things out. Why couldn't this marriage work after all these years and with both of us serving in ministry?

As the marriage difficulties continued, I cried out to God for a stronger prayer life. I joined a prayer group, attended prayer meetings and prayer services. My mother-in-law would spend countless hours on the telephone and in person, pouring into me spiritually. She bought me several types of spiritual books, bibles and spent countless hours teaching me the Word of God. We formulated a great relationship despite it all. She taught me to hope and trust in God, because miracles do happen. Our relationship grew despite my failing marriage. She is a cancer survivor who was only given 6 months to live. But despite a grim prognosis she is still alive 25 years later. Surely, I believed God would do the same for my marriage.

I changed my lifestyle, no longer using drugs, drinking, or smoking cigarettes. Surely, I believed if I gave it all up to be used by God, He would heal my marriage. *God does not make deals*. He knows what we are going through, and His will is going to be done, especially if you are crying out to Him for help.

Approximately two years before my divorce, my oldest daughter, had a rash with non-specific symptoms. She was diagnosed with Systemic Lupus Erythematosus (SLE), a complex autoimmune disease, with Nephritis (affected the kidneys). There are several forms of Lupus, with SLE as the worst. SLE is an inflammatory disease caused when the immune system attacks its own tissues and with lupus that had already affected the kidneys. A kidney biopsy was needed to determine how badly the kidneys were affected and dialysis was needed as part of the treatment plan. My God, my daughter was only 16 with such a big disease. The treatment plan started with doses of steroids and multiple medications. The dose of steroids was so high, causing a moon face and weight gain; her dress size increased by 5 sizes in two months.

I discussed my faith with the doctor, telling her I believed in healing. The doctor smiled and restated, "there is no cure for lupus." Because of the increase in my faith, I began declaring healing over my daughter, anointing her with oil, over and over, until she was better.

Not only was I faced with the challenge of a failing marriage and a sick daughter, but on one occasion I went to the hospital without an insurance card. My husband said we did not have any insurance that year because he'd taken us (me and the girls) off the insurance plan. We went to the emergency department. My daughter was admitted, and I incurred over $11,000.00 for the hospital stay. I had no idea how I was going to pay the bill. I discussed my current financial situation with the social worker at the hospital. I asked if I was eligible for medical assistance. I cried out to God, "You said You would supply my need, according to Your riches and glory though Christ Jesus. This is a need, not a want." Two weeks later the social worker called informing me the bill had been taken care of.

I began to see miracle after miracle and my faith was continually increasing and growing. One day I was looking through some papers and stumbled upon the insurance cards with coverage for the girls and myself. We all had coverage for the time my husband said we were not covered. Why did I have to go through this test?

Thank God, I trusted Him and was living by His Word, even though I was hurting. My thoughts were redirected, remembering I was dealing with spirits, principalities, and wickedness; therefore, I had to use my faith to do spiritual warfare. I learned to battle for my daughters healing, to stand, and believe God. I took the lemons of my life and begin to make lemonade, becoming a warrior and a spiritual example for my girls.

Although my marriage was falling apart I continued to do what I was supposed to do. I kept a clean house, I cooked, did all the necessary chores, despite the situation. I never stopped taking care of home. This is where a lot of people mess up. They want to stop doing what is right when things are not going the way they feel it should go. If a person mistreats you, that does not give you the right or power and authority to mistreat them. What are you doing behind closed doors when no one is looking? Are you doing what God wants you to do or mistreating others because they have mistreated you?

This will always be a testing point. This is a furnace experience we must all go through. The question is, will you allow God to show you yourself or will you continue to look at the wrongs of others?

I knew I was being tested and tried, but I also knew I needed healing. Upon this knowledge, I moved to a new ministry and sat down from ministry to receive healing. I had all kinds of healing to go through - emotional, physical, and spiritual. I was drained from believing God would heal my marriage yet, it ended in divorce. During the divorce proceedings, my daughter was in remission from Lupus and gone away to college at the University of Southern Louisiana while my youngest daughter no longer lived at home. Here I am, living in a twelve-room house, all by myself. I knew God was trying to get my attention and later realized He was separating me unto Himself. He needed me to hear Him clearly, to understand what He had in store for me and the ministry He called me to.

I did not operate in ministry for two years. I sat and listened to the Word of God and began healing. Shortly after 2 years, He told me it was time to get back up again and serve in ministry. For five years I was in ministerial training, serving faithfully. I attended Bible College and every aspect of training that was required. I never felt accepted in the ministry I was presently attending. I never felt like a part of the team, but I continued obeying God's assignment for me. I kept pressing and encouraging myself in the Lord. There is nothing worse than serving in a ministry for years without feeling like you are a part of the family. I was only asked to minister one time, I preached *"Chosen and Made In The Furnace of Afflictions."* Later, I transferred to the Baton Rouge location as an extra mile member. I thank God for the move. There I felt like a part of the team. I felt like a family member and was used in multiple capacities at that location.

Two Sundays before Hurricane Katrina hit Louisiana, I had to minister. I remember the topic of my sermon was "We Have Been Assigned to Rebuild." I did not realize my message was prophetic. It was speaking to a group of people whom God would mandate to come back home and rebuild after one of the greatest disasters in American history. There was only a specific group of people whose steps would be ordered back to New Orleans to rebuild. This was a specific call and mandate given by God to a special group of people. I did not realize, I would also have the assignment to help women "Rebuild their lives one Miracle at A Time" in a 7 month live in transformation program.

Many people were displaced into various parts of the country after this disaster. Many people were fleeing for their lives and lost everything they owned. Almost everyone in my family lost every possession. Even my uncle lost his life in the storm because he did not evacuate.

There seemed to be one furnace after another. I found myself starting my life over in Houston, Texas; a city unfamiliar to me. I had no friends, and no family, with the exception, of my daughters and my niece. This truly was a furnace experience that I did not want to experience, but it was part of the plan of being **CHOSEN**.

The stress of losing everything you had, moving to a new state, and starting all over from scratch, was more than my oldest daughter could handle. Her lupus became active due to stress, and she began to experience kidney failure. The week Hurricane Katrina hit she was scheduled to have another kidney biopsy in New Orleans. The doctors in New Orleans had continually talked about putting her on dialysis. I had been praying and fasting that she would not have to undergo such a serious treatment. Today, I thank God for the transition to Houston. She was hospitalized, and instead of putting her on dialysis, the doctor agreed she was too young, he opted to try a form of chemotherapy, (Cytoxin) treatments. She was scheduled for 6 months of chemotherapy. Each treatment for six months, would require hospitalization for two days and high doses of steroids.

As victims of Katrina, we were given temporary Medicaid for three months. The very first chemo treatment was covered under the temporary Medicaid. When we went back for the 2nd treatment we were turned away because she no longer had coverage. The hospital refused to admit her unless we provided $3,500.00 each month for the next 5 months to receive continued treatments. I began to seek God for help and direction. Again, I cried out to God, "You said You would supply our need. You have done it before God and I know You are going to do it again." Now the burden of not just walking by faith for me, but to encourage my daughter to believe that He would come through for her. Needing financial assistance, I reached out to our state representative in Louisiana, also reaching out to the state officials of Texas. I contacted the Lupus foundation and other organizations I believed could provide the necessary assistance. One day I received a phone call from the office of the Senator of Texas. I explained in full detail the situation, making him aware we were Hurricane Katrina victims, we lost our jobs and health insurance prior to the storm, and we could not return home due to the loss of our homes, jobs, and benefits. Immediately his office helped us to expedite services for her to receive the medical attention she needed. *My God did it again!* She completed the remaining treatments which were successful in replenishing her kidney cells.

This was yet another furnace experience where our faith was being tested, yet, He was standing right there with us in the middle of the fire. Those fires helped me to understand God at an even greater level than before. No one could tell me God was not faithful. At this point in my life, I found myself going through these furnaces alone without friends or family. Just God and me alone.

When you stop and look at where life has taken you thus far. You can see you have experienced test, trials, and many fires. BUT GOD has been faithful to you. "**BUT GOD**"! Two three-letter words are God's only response to Satan's attacks and challenges. No matter what the intention of people or the enemy, whether good or bad, God will work it for your good. When your back is up against the wall and major decisions need to be made, you must have faith like Shadrach, Meshach, and Abednego. They were faced with being thrown into the fiery furnace, but they knew God was well able to deliver them. Look at the meaning of their names.

Shadrach means – **Jehovah has favored**
Meshach means – **Like God**
Abednego means – **Jehovah aides**

God has favored you to become more like Him and will aid you when you are in need. You must remember these things when going through your furnace experiences. The same thing He did for Shadrach, Meshach, and Abednego, He will do for you.

Daniel 3:8-21 gives us the perfect example of going through the fiery furnace and having victory to make it through. (Read **Daniel Chapter 3**). I want to reiterate some of the key elements mentioned in the Introduction with reference to Shadrach, Meshach, and Abednego.

FAITH is the key element to make it through the furnace. Verse 16 shows they knew their deliverer. Do you know who will deliver you through your furnace? Your faith will be tested, to see who will deliver you from the fire. It will be your **FAITH** and the promise of God's **Word** that will deliver you. Their response was, **BUT IF NOT, I WILL NOT SERVE ANY OTHER GOD** (v.18). You will have to take this stance also. You must declare that you will not serve another god or turn back, but you will trust God.

When you are going through, can you really stand on the Word of God? Shadrach, Meshach, and Abednego's faith were being tested at this point. They decided in their hearts to know and believe God was well able to deliver them, but if not, they were going to still trust Him and His will for their lives. What they were saying, at that moment was "for God I live and for God I die." You will need **unwavering FAITH** when going through your fiery trials. **YOU NEED TO KNOW WHAT GOD TOLD YOU, SHOWN YOU AND PROMISED YOU, WILL NOT CHANGE.** The only thing that will change is the way you look at what you are going through and keeping the proper perspective while going through it. His Word says, He will do it, if you but **BELIEVE**!

FOCUS is the next element you need while going through your furnace experience. Verse 23 displays this. Can you keep your focus while your flesh is being crucified? Can you still worship God? Can you still read your Word? Can you still pray? Can you still speak those things that be not as though they were? Right in the middle of your fiery furnace experience? The Scriptures says they fell down, bound, in the midst of the furnace. I believe they were worshipping God, in the midst, of the fire. Can you worship God in the middle of your fiery trials? You must keep your focus on God and not the fire. Can you hear the Scriptures coming out of your belly more than the trial you are faced with? Who is speaking the loudest; your spirit man or your flesh? It is imperative that you keep your focus.

ENDURANCE is another element you must possess. Verse 28 shows great endurance by Shadrach, Meshach, and Abednego. They yielded their bodies and trusted God. They submitted, surrendered, and gave of themselves totally to God. It says the furnace was turned up seven times hotter. **James 1:12** says, *"Blessed is the man that endureth temptation: for when he is tried, he shall receive the crown of life, which the Lord hath promised to them that love him."*

God is trying to create great people, but great people go through great trials and tribulations. He is molding and shaping you, so that He can use you to help His people. It is not about you and it is not about me. It is about what God can do through you and me for His people.

So, I encourage you not to give up. Do not quit but endure to the end. **Romans 12:12** says, *"Rejoicing in hope; patient in tribulation; continuing instant in prayer."* It was not until they began to worship, in the middle of the fiery trial, that they were set free from the things that had them bound. They were able to see God was right there all along. I could just imagine they were saying, "God I know You are here with us and we are still going to worship You." This is the place where the enemy and those who did you wrong realize that God is with you. They will see that God protected, healed, and delivered you. Deliverance from every fiery trial, every test, is what will come when you endure hardness as a good soldier **(II Tim. 2:3)**. Verses 26 and 27 of Daniel 3 shows how the enemy wanted Shadrach, Meshach, and Abednego to believe after he turned the heat up seven times hotter, it was the end for them. This did not stop them from worshipping God. The king soon realized there was someone else keeping them safe in the middle of the fire. This is our ultimate example of what and how we should be in the middle of our trials. Yes, God will set a table for you in the presence of your enemies **(Psa. 23:5)**. Once they see it could not destroy you, they will want to take a closer look at what kept you sane in the fire. This will make a believer out of them or make them curious to see what kind of God you serve. Your testimony will let them know your God did it for you. It now becomes a reality, your God is real, and He really does love you. *Verse 28* shows that Shadrach, Meshach, and Abednego received their deliverance.

You will also receive your deliverance if you have **FAITH**, **FOCUS**, and **ENDURANCE**. You will have a great **TESTIMONY** that no one can take from you. From that point on your **TESTIMONY** will become a part of your ministry to share with others so they, too, will have hope in the midst, of their trials.

One thing I love about God, He assures us through **James 1:3**, *"Knowing this, that the trying of your faith worketh patience. But let patience have her perfect work, that ye may be perfect and entire, wanting nothing."* He promises trouble doesn't last always. I love that about my God. Once we come out of our furnace experience, it will always be followed by Promotion. Yes, promotion. In Verse 30, Shadrach, Meshach, and Abednego were promoted. It is promotion time for those who have been through the fire and have passed the test.

Look at Job. He lost everything, was ridiculed, talked about, and mistreated. **"BUT GOD"** delivered and promoted him. He received greater than what he had before. **Job 23:10** states, *"But he knoweth the way that I take: when he hath tried me, I shall come forth as gold."* If you look at the book of Job, it was the 23rd chapter. The number 23 represents death and the number 10 represents testimony. After going through his fiery trials and dying to his flesh, he had an awesome **TESTIMONY.**

Jesus Christ, our ultimate example of Faith, Focus, Endurance, Deliverance, and Testimony, is all summed up in **Hebrews 12:2**, *"Looking unto Jesus, the author and finisher of our faith; who for the joy that was set before him endureth the cross, despising the shame, and is set down at the right hand of the throne of God."* **THOSE WHO HAVE BEEN THROUGH THE FURNACE** will have to go through something. **DEAD MEN DON'T HAVE FEELINGS.** When your flesh dies, you are not moved by everything which comes to test you. God is a consuming fire. He burns up everything not like Him. God is only trying to kill your flesh. He is not trying to kill you.

There is someone reading this book right now and you are in the middle of a fiery trial and you do not understand why. God is doing a work in you. He is shaping, molding, and purifying you. Maybe you are about to go through a fiery trial, God is preparing you to better understand what and why you are going through. Finally, you have been tested and tried, you have learned a lot about yourself and God through this process. Now it is time to come out of the furnace. You passed the test. After reading this book, you will have a better understanding of what God is doing in and through your life.

REMEMBER YOU ARE "CHOSEN AND MADE IN THE FURNACE OF AFFLICTIONS"!!!!!

Chapter Three

LOSING TO WIN

"But whatever things were gain to me, those things I have counted as loss for the sake of Christ" **(Philippians 1:21)**

$\mathcal{N}$obody likes to lose. Vince Lombardi, coach of the Green Bay Packers said, "To some winning isn't everything, it is the only thing." It is interesting how much winning and losing plays an important part in our daily life. Those who are caught up in the things of the world, worship winners. According to the world's standards, they see most of us as losers. As a Christian we can not be consumed with possessions and accomplishments to determine if we are winning or losing. Our life is hidden in Christ. Some have lost loved ones, jobs, possessions, and positions.

Paul knew all too well about this. After his conversion, Ananias delivered a word from the LORD to him concerning the great things he must suffer for the sake of Christ's name **(Acts 9:16)**. He would later suffer through shipwreck, stonings, beatings and afflictions to his body. He suffered the loss of all things, yet GOD caused him to triumph over and through every one of them. Paul declared, *"I reckoned that the sufferings of this present time are not worthy to be compared with the glory which shall be revealed in us"* **(Romans 8:18)**.

It doesn't matter what your process is, it can't be compared to the sufferings of **JESUS CHRIST**. When we get so consumed in our process, we selfishly forget what **JESUS** suffered. I've tried to accept and deal with my process and constantly remind myself that no pain, no suffering, is as great as what **JESUS** suffered. There are stages along the way and lessons to be learned, but nothing compares to His loss. To follow **CHRIST** is to move into areas unknown to us and lean on HIM for guidance. The spiritual process is working out what GOD has already worked in us. This process is very critical. HE needs to see the type of fruit you will bear during the process. At times, our fruit will be pruned, tested, and put on display. External appearances are often deceptive; we know how to look a certain way to make everyone think everything is good. The Word of God says that *"He looks at the heart"* **(I Sam. 16:7)**. Our inner man, the spirit man is going through the process.

Our spiritual process will test areas of obedience, faith, patience, courage, wisdom, service, humility, forgiveness, and love. **Mark 8:34-35** says, *"...Whosoever will come after Me, let him deny himself, and take up his cross, and follow Me. For whosoever will save his life shall lose it; but whosoever shall lose his life for My sake and the gospel's, the same shall save it."*

Timing is also a significant part of the process. Like fruit on a vine, there is a certain time fruit grows and there is a time when you see nothing. We need to learn patience with GOD and ourselves as we wait for the harvest of fruit. We will go through a pruning process, where GOD removes and cuts away unwanted parts of the flesh, He also cuts away people who will only be with you for a certain season. I always say don't hold onto things and people so tight that if God calls you cannot let go of them.

I am reminded of the time I was getting licensed to preach. My marriage was falling apart. It should have been an exciting time, but my private life was falling apart while my ministry was coming forth. I questioned God and asked Him **"why now?"** He said to me, **"If not now, when? Are you going to answer the call now?"** I tried to get out of it, feeling ashamed, but my Pastor, at the time, told me he was going to be obedient to God's instructions.

My husband was the musician for my licensing ceremony. This was a special blessing for me because I got licensed with my sister, who had prayed for me when I was living an ungodly lifestyle. Now God was allowing her and I to be licensed together. Just about the time we were to receive our license, my husband walked out of the church. It was such a bittersweet moment. I was in the fire once again. I could not even enjoy what was to be a memorable event, not having my husband to celebrate with me.

There were so many things happening at this point in my life. I had to be healed of emotional scars, rejection, and loneliness. I was married, yet so lonely. I found myself more alone than ever before. I understand there is a time God separates you unto Himself. Separation, by no means, feels good, but it is something that God requires in the life of those He choose. I knew I was going through a major transition in my life. One that was so un-comfortable, but, yet so real. All I could think of was holding on to God's unchanging hand.

It seems like many fires were burning in my life. I had been recently laid off my job and my relationship with my husband was failing. Two weeks after I found a new job, my husband served me with divorce papers. Although I knew our marriage was in trouble, I believed God could fix it. It bothered me when we began the separation of property, court battles and property settlements. I felt as if this was a dream and I had been stripped of everything I worked so hard to gain over the last 12 years of my life. Once the property was settled, I did not see him again for many years.

Over time I had to forgive, release the hurt, the pain, and the bitterness. The wounds of my heart needed to be healed. With the help of the Holy Spirit that did happen. I had to submerge myself into the Word of God. I attended prayer meetings, focused on specific areas of the Word to help me, and read spiritual books related to my situation. It required my undivided attention to receive and maintain my healing. As I began receiving healing in my spirit, my heart, my emotions and in my mind, I was able to move forward and live again. I began to smile again and enjoy my new walk with God.

It was 2 ½ years after my divorce that I met someone. We dated about a year and then we were married. We had a small, simple ceremony in our pastor's office. I thought my life was going in the right direction. I would finally be happy. We were both serving God, had purchased a new home, and a fresh start. We had everything we desired, or so I thought. Truth be told, looking back, God always displays warning signs when things are not right.

The night before I was to get married, I opened the Word to read and pray. My eyes went to Isaiah 54:5, *"For thy Maker is thy husband; the Lord of hosts is his name; and thy Redeemer the Holy One of Israel: The God of the whole earth shall he be called."* I did not take this passage of Scripture as a personal word but dismissed what the Holy Spirit was saying to me. The very next morning I opened the Word to read and pray and the same exact Scripture was opened to me. I asked **God "What are You saying to me?"** A part of me knew, but a part of me wanted to go on with my plans. After you have been married for 12 years and had been with that person a total of 14 years, it is hard to think that you would even date again, let alone marry. Now I was given an opportunity to be married again and I did not want to forfeit that marriage.

The Bible tells us to know those that labor among you. I belonged to a prayer group of powerful women. I had known these ladies for years. I knew their commitment to the Lord, their love for God and knew the Holy Spirit dwelled in them. One of the ladies kept calling me and pleading with me not to marry him. She kept begging me as often as she would reach out to me, not to do this. Now I see that she was sent with a warning by God. I felt in my heart she just did not want to see me happy. I knew she was a woman of God and I began to get angry because I could not believe she wasn't happy for me. Of course, I now know that this was a trick from the enemy.

One day she called again. I knew what she wanted. This day I asked her to tell me why she felt the way she did. She revealed to me a dream. God had shown her the both of us in the dream. After hearing the details of the dream, I did not want to believe this dream was real or it would happen to me. Ultimately, in the end, he would turn his back on me and I was wounded again. I was like the children of Israel. The Lord told them He was their king. It was not good enough for them, they wanted a new king (Saul). Saul was their ultimate downfall. So was my marriage. God allowed me to marry, it was my will. God attempted to assure me He was my husband but, I ignored it. It turned out as time progressed I eventually began to see how true it was.

A downward spiral began in my life and I started losing everything I worked hard to gain. I was laid off my job, separated from my husband and a multitude of things in my life were failing. I began to seek God for my life and direction of what to do. Instead of working for someone else, I was given the vision to open a staffing agency. God directed me to go forth, to step out in faith. He did not tell me to take on a business partner, but I did so I would have enough resources for the business. Once again, I still did not have the courage to trust God for the provisions of the business. He gave me the vision, I should have trusted Him for the provision. In the beginning, it was a struggle to obtain starting capital. Eventually a door was opened to obtain the necessary funding. This proved to be another bittersweet time in my life. My marriage had ended, but the business was birthed.

Again, I found myself moving back to my parents' home. I was ashamed of my failed marriages. My parents had been married almost 50 years and I was going through another divorce. I was embarrassed and felt defeated. I could not imagine what my parents and family were thinking about my life. This was not the example that was set before me. As a Christian, and a minister, I could not get my life together. I was serving in ministry, going to Bible college, and now going through another painful divorce.

Once I moved back into my parents' home, I decided to return my car to the bank, instead of allowing the bank to come and repossess it. I had purchased my dream car after my property settlement from my previous divorce. Financing the business was great and two cars was not necessary. I was going through many trials, one after another, which pushed me into the face of God. I was seeking to stay close and know the very heartbeat of God for my life, at this time.

> **Philippians 3:7** says, *"But what things were gain to me, these I have counted loss for Christ, yet indeed I also count all things loss for the excellence of the knowledge of Christ Jesus my Lord, for whom I have suffered the loss of all things, and count them as dung, that I may gain Christ."*

I lost my pride, my possessions and myself due to disobedience. I faced embarrassment, and loss only to be awakened and to see the real picture. **I HAD TO LOSE TO WIN.** Lose in the Greek means **"to put to death."** I had to crucify my flesh and my fleshly desires. This pivotal point in my life would be the beginning of a spiritual process that would take place for years to come.

The first thing I had to do to get back on my feet was to take **INVENTORY**. John 12:24-26 says, *"Verily, verily, I say unto you, except a corn of wheat fall into the ground and die, it abideth alone; but if it die, it bringeth forth much fruit. He that loveth his life shall lose it; and he that hateth his life in this world shall keep it unto life eternal."*

It was time for me to face reality; I had messed up. I had put man before God. He told me He was my husband, but I wanted a natural husband. Now it was time to face the consequences. I had to take inventory, I had to acknowledge I was carrying weights and wounds I needed to get rid of. **FACE REALITY. IN ORDER, TO WIN, YOU ARE GOING TO HAVE TO LOSE SOME THINGS.** What things are you holding on to so tightly that it could risk you losing everything? What things are you looking at so much that will hinder your view and vision of what you really need to see? Is it yourself or an idol that has become a distraction, a mate, a job, a title or position, friends, fame, or fortune? Even becoming a new convert, you cannot stay in the world and totally come to Christ. Is it a bad habit, an addiction, a hidden secret, un-forgiveness, greed, or power?

We need to face reality and move forward. We cannot continue to look back at our past failures. It keeps us stagnate and stuck. At times we will experience being blindsided or blinded, sometimes to people or things and sometimes to our accomplishments. The old saying is, "You can't move forward looking in the rearview mirror." Wake up now, arise and see you have a chance to get it right.

Fear and the fear of failing tried to overtake me. I began telling myself that there is no way I can make it, after going through these test and trials. I was ashamed, full of sorrow and embarrassment. What kind of example was I in the eyes of my daughters? What did my peers in ministry think about my failed marriages and my losses? Fear cripples you and diminishes your self-image. The longer fear lives in your heart the greater the challenge gets. There are times we need to admit we took the wrong turn and now we need to repent, re-evaluate, stop, reroute, and start over. It is OK to fail sometimes, but you should learn through your failures. Failure is not the end. It is a learning tool to help you get back up and start over the right way.

Yes, I know the job folded, the marriage did not work, the business closed, but it does not mean you are a failure. My business partner left because the pressures of business were too great to handle. She left. The debt and responsibilities of the business fell on me. I looked to God and remembered He told me to start the business, I chose to include someone as a business partner, thinking we would be more secure, and share the responsibility. The one thing I attempted to avoid, happened, all the responsibility fell on me. We were not equally yoked in faith. We learn from our mistakes. Get up and start over again. Let God arise in you. Carry His spirit and be not consumed with "I failed." Realize who you are in Christ. Make sure Christ, the King of Glory, lives in you. With that knowledge, you can get up and start over again.

There may be some relationships you need to let go of. **LET GO, LET GO, LET GO!** My former pastor said if people are not adding to you, they are depleting you or weighing you down. They may have helped in the past and you may feel indebted to them, but this is a new season, so let go. Some people are like leeches and don't ever want to let go. Pull them off and keep moving. There are some people who want to control your life; trying to hold you back, speaking negativity in your life. They are sent to discourage and distract the plan and purpose of God in your life. Lastly, there are those trying to go where God is taking you, to a place they are not called. **LET GO, LET GO, LET GO!** Die to yourself, your flesh, and those people who are holding you back. Do not make any more excuses, just be **obedient**. **Luke 14:26-27** says, *"If any man come to me, and hate not his father, and mother, and wife, and children, and brethren, and sisters, yea, and his own life also, he cannot be my disciple. And whosoever doth not bear his cross, and come after me, cannot be my disciple."*

Abraham had to lay down his only son on the altar. Jesus had to lay down His life for you and I to have the right to the Tree of Life. He lost His life, so we might have life. Ask God for the grace to determine who and what to keep in your life and who and what to get rid of. Grasp the courage to let go. Paul realized all his accomplishments were **nothing,** but dung and he lost all he had to win knowledge, wisdom, understanding and a relationship with Jesus Christ. He had to gain knowledge of Christ as a Savior, deliverer, healer, protector, guide, counselor, and redeemer. **I realized I had to lose to win. I had to lose pride, disobedience, selfish motives, and possessions to gain the life I needed to live in Christ.**

WHAT ARE YOU WILLING TO LOSE IN ORDER THAT YOU MAY WIN?????

THE PROCESS IS NECESSARY

"Many Are the afflictions of the righteous, but God delivereth him out of them all." **Psalm 34:19**

$\mathcal{T}$here is a process we must go through, in order, for our character to become pleasing in GOD's sight. All believer's will go through a process, not all at the same time and not all in the same way. The key to the spiritual process is staying faithful while going through your journey. It is about abiding in **CHRIST** and learning to practice **HIS** principles while in the process.

Many people don't know how or where the process will take them. Our fundamental choice as Christians should be to get to know **JESUS** intimately and allow the **HOLY SPIRIT** to transform us into **HIS** image. **Philippians 3:10** declares, *"That I might know HIM, and the power of HIS resurrection, and the fellowship of HIS sufferings; being made conformable to HIS death"*

Most of us at one time or another have had a dream to do something big for God, but what can happen is our dream can be put to sleep or die in the midst, of the process. Believe it, or not, all of us will go through a process. The enemy will try to weigh you down with burdens, trials, and thoughts to get us side-tracked or quit.

Shortly, after moving back home with my parents, my father had a massive stroke. It was so serious the doctors prepared us for the possibility of placing him on life support. My father was asked if he wanted to be put on life support in the event his organs shut down. I will never forget the look on his face; he never answered, he just turned his head. It reminded me of the biblical account of King Hezekiah when he turned his face to the wall and cried to God. My father never responded to the medical staff and they did not have to place him on life support. However, he went through grueling months of rehab. He remained paralyzed on the left side of his entire body. Before the stroke he was a very vibrant man who exercised 3 times a day. A retired letter carrier with 35 years of service, had only retired 3 years before the massive stroke. Not long after having the stroke, he was diagnosed with cancer of the prostrate. Our lives had changed drastically, but we had matured in the Lord and we began praying and interceding for his healing. He received radiation, which proved to be successful.

We had grown and matured in the Word of God. My sisters and I were raised Catholic and we attended Catholic schools. As we grew older, my sister began studying the Bible. As Catholics, we were never taught to study the Bible. Everything we learned was printed in the weekly missalette. As she continued to study the Bible, she grew spiritually, and she began interceding for me to be set free. I know her prayers and the death of my friend brought me to a place of salvation. We attended church together and began to grow in ministry.

We attended a small ministry in the St. Bernard Housing Project; where true ministry went forth. We helped illiterate children, poor and hurting people who were oppressed, depressed and in bondage. It was here that my drug ministry began. I began teaching biblical 12-step classes to people in the community. I was licensed to preach and ordained in this ministry. It taught me true compassion and how to love people who needed to be loved. This gave me the opportunity to work side-by-side with my sister in ministry. We cooked hot meals every day, fed the children, tutored, and taught them spiritual lessons to apply in their lives. On the weekends, we washed the little girls' hair in the community and helped them with special needs. It was a blessing to serve together in ministry. This was the epitome of true ministry for me.

We must be prepared for change because nothing stays the same. My sister married and moved to a new ministry and later we were separated because of Hurricane Katrina. One Sunday as I was leaving church, the Holy Spirit said, "you will not pass this way again". I asked the Holy Spirit what did that mean? The following Sunday we were heading to Houston, Texas because Hurricane Katrina was headed to New Orleans. My life was never the same again. This was a furnace that many of us had to go through.

Guess what? I was right where God wanted me to be; I was in the perfect will of God, yet my faith was being put to the ultimate test again. You might feel like your life is being tested right now, like never, before. Just like the children of Israel had found themselves at the Red Sea, faced with what looked like an impossible situation, the enemy behind them and the Red Sea before them, I found myself in a similar position with nowhere to go. I was in a state of emergency.

I was in a big and unfamiliar city. My daughters and I had left everything we owned in New Orleans. I was unprepared for Hurricane Katrina. My oldest daughter had been in the hospital earlier that week and the latter part of the week my youngest daughter was involved in a car accident. When I finally found out that a hurricane was coming to New Orleans, I had only one day to prepare. I did not pack the right clothes, took about 3 outfits, believing in my heart we would be back in a few days. When the Holy Spirit said that I would never pass that way again, He meant it. While driving to Houston I passed a sign that said **CROSSOVER.** I did not realize the significance of that sign at the time. I lived in Houston for 2 years before moving to back to New Orleans.

Sometimes it seems like your problems are so big; there is no sign of relief. The enemy will whisper to you and tell you it is foolish to trust God; he will tell you it is no good to have faith. He'll tell you that your marriage is going to fall apart, your finances will never improve, your health will continue to deteriorate, your children will never live right, you will never find the right job, you will never write that book, you should get out of ministry because your life will never line up with the ministry God has called you to. I struggled because these were the very things that the enemy told me. The City of New Orleans and other states had experienced the same disaster. Many people were displaced, families split up, people lost homes, jobs, and everything they owned. This gave me the tenacity to not quit and give up. I began to see people lose hope, lose their lives, because of the great devastation brought on by Hurricane Katrina. I did not understand why we went through this, but I knew this was not my end.

I had to first recognize God's purpose. The events of our lives do not happen just because; God is in control of everything. The name **Katrina** means **cleansing**. I knew God was cleaning up our city and for some of us we would come out better than before Katrina. God was shifting people, changing situations for some and opening doors for others. Sometimes we feel like we are being punished for something we may have done wrong or we made God mad. When we face our own furnace, that place of overwhelming difficulty, we tend to believe We had it coming. This is not the kind of God we serve. When we face certain difficulties, we should realize God wants to get the glory and He is teaching us to trust Him. He knows your faith is being tested. He knows when you feel like quitting and giving up. **Isaiah 43:2** says, *"When thou passest through the waters, I will be with thee; and through the rivers, they shall not overtake thee; when thou walkest through the fire, thou shalt not be burned; neither shall the flame kindle upon thee."*

The furnace of Katrina brought me into a closer relationship with God. I had to posture myself to be still and listen to what God was telling me to do and go where He directed me to go. He knew it was painful, and at times it kept me awake at night. I will never forget, three days after New Orleans filled with water, we knew we were not going home anytime soon. My cousin and I discussed how we needed to check out of the hotel and put my parents on a plane to California. My dad had just completed radiation and he needed to be in a stable environment. I will never forget how my mother cried at the airport as we all had to part ways. It seemed like everything my mother had held back since my father's stroke had come out in a desperate cry that day. She did not want us to split up, but the Holy Spirit was not releasing me to leave Houston. How heartbreaking it was. Everyone in the airport turned around to see what was going on. The emotional scene left others in tears.

The drive back to the hotel for me and my cousin was one of silent agony. My parents had never lived anywhere else but New Orleans and now they found themselves hundreds of miles away from their children and grandchildren. God knew how painful it was. He saw the stress, and strain of it all. He saw the tears I shed when I was alone, but He kept reminding me to be strong for my family. Now I had to stand up and really tread in territory I had never been before.

One morning, as my girls and I went to breakfast at a nearby IHOP, my cousin who had been missing due to the storm, called saying he had been on a rooftop of his apartment complex for days before he was rescued. We cried for joy. Little did we know there was a pastor and his wife sitting near our booth. They heard our conversation and came over and invited us to their church across the parking lot to get some toiletries and clothes. As we approached the church, the name of their church was **"New Beginnings."** I remember weeping at the sight of the name of the church because God was speaking loud and clear to me. Fear gripped my heart, but deep down I said, **"Yes Lord, I hear You."** This was going to be a faith walk for sure.

My granddaughter was running a fever at the time of our visit to the church. The pastor made a phone call to a doctor's office and scheduled an appointment for us immediately. It was 45 minutes away to the doctor's office, in a city where we did not know our way around. The employees in the office treated her for strep throat, and gave us medication free of charge and collected $500.00 amongst them to give to us. We wept in that doctor's office because we saw the hand of God move on our behalf. He began to show me I was on a faith walk like I had never seen. He whispered to me, *"Know I got you. Just trust Me."* He says, *"For my thoughts are not your thoughts, neither are your ways my ways, saith the LORD"* **(Isaiah 55:8).**

When we are faced with terrifying situations, it is so easy to lose our perspective. Too often when confronted with an impossible situation, rather than dealing with it head on, we want to take the easy way out. We say, "I don't want to deal with this, I don't want to fight so I'll just quit." Someone reading this might feel that if things don't get any better, you are going to quit. You say you are going to stop going to church, stop reading your Word, stop praying, and you just want to give up on God.

You should trust God even though you feel this way, and you believe there is no way out. God has a great plan for you, just as He had a great plan for me and my family. He doesn't want you to run from your crisis, He wants you to meet it head on with courage. He is going to see you through. There is nothing too hard for God. There were people who had never left New Orleans before; they didn't survive. Not because they were caught in the storm, they did not know how to handle being misplaced, alone and not knowing how to call on the Lord for help. They had no idea of the promises of God. They were faced with hopelessness, grief, and helplessness. You must know the Lord that says, *"Be still and know I am God"* **(Psalm 46:10)**. He promises He will fight for you; you only need to be still. We must stand still and focus on God's promises.

I could have focused on the fact that I lost everything, we were homeless, and my entire family lost their homes, or the loss of the life of one of my uncles. But, all I could do was stand on God's Word. I began to devour the Word for direction, clarity, peace, guidance and understanding. His Word ordered my footsteps to divine connections I needed in the middle of the trauma.

God strengthened me and helped me to find the resources needed for my daughter's healing. He enabled me to drive my parents van to California and set up their new apartment. He gave me wisdom to find an organization to help rebuild my parents' home. He strengthened and covered me countless times traveling alone, back, and forth while driving on the highway to take care of the rebuilding process of their home. Oh, yes God kept me, I didn't lose my mind. He made a way out of no way for me. Yes, He did. I came to understand why He did it.

1 Samuel 12:22 (NKJV) says, *"For the LORD will not forsake His people, for His great name's sake, because it has pleased the LORD to make you His people."* **I was Chosen and Made in the Furnace of These Afflictions.**

God is committed to His people and to Himself. **Isaiah 48:9** says, *"For my name's sake will I defer mine anger, and for my praise I will refrain for thee, that I cut thee not off."* God cares about the worth of His own reputation and He will not allow you to be down for long. Can you look at how you have been tested, or being tested now? Your patience, your love, your faithfulness, your motives, your loyalty, your health, your relationships, your finances, and your families are being tested. **The furnace is designed to remove impurities and to produce fruit.** For His name's sake, He is going to make a way. For His name's sake, He is going to heal you. For His name's sake, He is going to deliver you. It may not be what you deserve, but it is what He promised through His Word.

"The Process is Necessary." It is the making of the vessel. Our lives are much like popcorn. It starts out as a hard kernel of corn, but it goes through intense heat and pressure before it explodes into the fullness of popcorn. Once it is popped it has a wonderful aroma and it tastes so good. In similar manner, there will be times when we all face the fiery furnace, the fiery trials that Peter refers to. It will be fiery circumstances that put our faith to the test, but in the end, it produces trust in God and brings glory to His name. It will make you a vessel of honor; not a vessel of dishonor.

Even the process of making bread can help us to understand the process of being **Called** and **Chosen**. If made from scratch, the first part of the process is the sifting. The flour goes through a sifting process to get the lumps out. There are times, as God's chosen, we are to be sifted so that the things not needed in our lives come to the surface. These are the things the Lord needs to deal with concerning us. He will begin to show us some things about ourselves, as we read His Word. He begins to teach us about not compromising, no longer going back and forth doing worldly things. He begins to sift us. We need to know the devil desires to sift us also. **Luke 22:31-32** says, *"And the Lord said, Simon, Simon, behold Satan hath desired to have you, that he may sift you as wheat; but I have prayed for thee that thy faith fail not, and when thou are converted, strengthen thy brethren."* It also represents sifting away selfish ambitions, and pride.

Just like Satan desired to have Peter, he desires to have you and I to sift us like wheat. He wants to separate us from God's plan and purpose for our lives.

Just as He prayed for Peter, Jesus Christ, our intercessor is praying for us, that our faith will not fail us. He gives us every opportunity to strengthen our faith by studying His Word, have a more consistent prayer life, fellowshipping along with other believers, and coming together to worship Him.

The next step is to mix the ingredients. This is the part of the process where He is teaching us how to be balanced; to grow and mature.

The **YEAST** – the balancing and leavening agent. This represents the **HOLY SPIRIT**. **Proverbs 11:1** says, *"A false balance is an abomination to the Lord. But a just weight is his delight."*

The **WATER** – represents the **WORD**. **Ephesians 5:26-27** says, *"That he might sanctify and cleanse it with the washing of water by the word. That he might present it to himself a glorious church, not having spot, or wrinkle, or any such thing; but that it should be holy and without blemish."*

The **SUGAR** – represents **FAITH. Romans 12:3** says, *"For I say, through the grace given unto me, to every man that is among you, not to think of himself more highly than he ought to think; but to think soberly, according as God hath dealt to every man a measure of faith."* **Hebrews 11:6** states, *"And without faith, it is impossible to please Him; for he that cometh to God must believe that he is, and that he is a rewarder of them that diligently seek him."*

The **SALT** – A purging and a purifying agent. God wants to purge, purify, and preserve us. **Philippians 2:13a,** *"Ye are the salt of the earth."*

All the ingredients are mixed together to bring balance and make a good blend. This becomes the foundation. **Luke 6:48**, *"He is like a man which built a house, and digged deep, and laid the foundation on a rock; and when the flood arose, the stream beat vehemently upon that house, and could not shake it; for it was founded upon a rock."* **1 Corinthians 3:1** says, *"For other foundation can no man lay than that is laid, which is Jesus Christ."*

The mixed ingredients are then placed on a floured surface and kneaded for 10 minutes. To keep from sticking, or falling apart, the floured surface will keep the dough at the proper consistency. This is the stage where

Jesus comes in to help us. The dough is then placed in a warm place until it rises twice in size. **James 1:3-4**, *"Knowing this, that the trying of your faith worketh patience. But let patience have her perfect work, that ye may be entire, wanting nothing."* You are now in a dark place, covered, but left hidden until you grow and mature. You must wait until your flesh dies, your faith increases, and you begin to mature. God uses this time to allow you to grow and rise in your new place. **Philippians 1:6** says, *"Being confident of this very thing, that he which hath begun a good work in you will perform it until the day of Jesus Christ."*

Once the bread has doubled in size, it is punched down again and placed on another floured surface. You may think you have been through enough already, you have grown and matured, but now there is still much more you must go through. **Luke 12:48b** says, *"For unto whomsoever much is given, of him shall be much required; and to whom man have committed much, of him they will ask the more."*

Just as things started getting better, it seemed like you were beginning to see the breaking of day, then here comes another trial; another fiery furnace. Positions change, reputations are on the line, relationships begin to fall apart, worldly ties are severed, and even some Christian ties fall apart. This time we are surviving solely on the grace and the mercy of God. This is when we must cling to the vine. We are being tested again to a greater level.

The bread now has to be kneaded 3 or 4 more times to remove air to prepare it for the oven. God is telling us, **"I'm trying to get your attention. You are not in the Word enough. You need to get more serious about your prayer life."** God wants us to make sure all the doors are closed from the enemy. Air pockets in the bread will prevent it from baking properly. This is indicative of us closing every door that could be open. We are to stay away from every appearance of evil. We need to make sure we are ready for the next phase of the process.

Isaiah 26:20 says, *"Come, my people, enter thou into thy chambers, and shut thy doors about thee: hide thyself as it were for a little moment, until the indignation be overpast."* God wants us to mature a little more, keep the door closed to the enemy that He may prepare us for our new post or position.

The next step of the process is to place the bread in an oiled pan. Oil represents the anointing. The anointing protects us; it keeps us from sticking and coming apart. It helps us to minister under the power of the Holy Spirit. At this point God will not allow us to get stuck in the same situation again. You shall not pass this way again. You will not have to deal with this situation again. This molding process represents God shaping us into something new for the next level and the next stages of our lives.

The bread stays in the pan until it rises. This is symbolic of the dawning of a new day, a new level in Christ, and a new anointing. At this stage, you should begin to get prophecies about your life to confirm what God has spoken to you. The Word declares to us in **Isaiah 43:18**, *"Remember ye not the former things, neither consider the things of old. Behold I will do a new thing: now it shall spring forth, shall ye not know it."* We are being built up and encouraged due to the prophecies, and the Word of God we read. Now we are able, to see some of them come to fruition.   We should understand that when we receive a word of prophecy, that word will be tried. **Psalm 18:30**, *"As for God, his way is perfect: the word of the Lord is tried: he is a buckler to all those who trust in him."* A buckler is a round shield to protect you. You will begin to experience circumstances that totally look like the opposite of what was spoken to you. God wants to see if you will stand on the promise of that word. **Will you believe what God has spoken even in tough times? Will you still believe when all hell is breaking loose? Psalm 12:6** says, *"The words of the Lord are pure words: as silver tried in a furnace of earth, purified seven times."* This is the time in your life when you must stand on the promise of God's Word and trust that it will happen.

Now it is time to place your mold in the oven (furnace) at 450 degrees for 40 minutes. That is intense heat. The number 40 represents tests, trials, and probation. Our test, trials and probation period may not be for 40 minutes like the time it takes for the baking of bread, it may be 4 years or what might seem like 40 years. When you go through the furnace experience, it may feel like you are all alone. **Job 23:8** says, *"Behold, I go forward, but he is not there; and backward, but cannot perceive him: on the left hand, where he doeth work, but cannot behold him: he hideth himself on the right hand, that I cannot see him."* You may find yourself in a dark place where the trials seem to keep coming and you're wondering when these trials will end. **1 Corinthians 10:13** says, *"There hath no temptation taken you, but such as is common to man: but God is faithful, who will not suffer you to be tempted above that ye are able; but with the temptation also make a way of escape that ye may be able to bear it."*

At the end of December 2013, God told me to put down everything I was doing in ministry as we came closer to the end of the year. In my mind, I kept reasoning with God that I would step down as soon as a task I had been working on was completed. How many of you know that you can't reason with God, especially when he tells you to do a certain thing? You would think that all I had been through already, I would obey. It does not matter how small or big a thing, obedience is better than sacrifice. So, I crossed over into the new year without making a change.

By the end of January 2014, I had become ill with severe abdominal pain. I made an appointment to see my doctor and he admitted me the same day for emergency surgery. The scans found I had a large mass under my liver and scar tissue from a previous surgery had wrapped around a few of my organs. It turned out that the mass was the size of a full-term baby, which meant I had a large incision. My Heavenly Father was good to me; it was not cancerous.

After surgery, I wanted to recover at my own house. I needed no distractions and to spend time with God to get an understanding of why this happened to me. One thing I had come to know is when I am going through a serious trial or fire, I need to get into a place where it is quiet, so I can talk to God and hear from Him.

God worked it out that my aunt from California came down to take care of me. It was a set up and was divinely orchestrated by God Himself. She did an awesome job taking care of me. I would see her spend hours in the Word daily, which helped me to stay in my Word and in a posture of prayer. She had a great sense of humor and kept me laughing. **Proverbs 17:22a** says, "A merry heart doeth good like a medicine". I needed her laughter and humor because God was dealing with me about being disobedient to what He had told me to do at the end of the previous year. Yet, He showed His faithfulness to me anyway. I repented and made the great decision I was supposed to make in December 2013. God is faithful, even when we are not.

My aunt spent countless hours talking with me and giving counsel to me on the matters I shared with her. As my body began to heal and I was back on my feet, she said she was going to stay in New Orleans for a while. However, one day I noticed she wasn't feeling well. I had never known her to be a sickly person. Even when she endured being physically burned over 60% of her body and had to stay in the hospital for nine months, going through multiple graphs and treatments, she handled it like a champion. She never let you know how much she truly suffered, for she was a strong woman who endured what it was like to literally go through the fire. She made it seem as if it was nothing. She became ill and was diagnosed with kidney, liver, and lung cancer. She only survived two weeks after being diagnosed. I had surgery January 29, 2014 and she was gone by March 27, 2014. God had sent her to me on a mission. Little did I know I would be a part of her final mission.

I was not even totally healed, and now my heart took another hit. I don't think I could truly explain to anyone how I was feeling at this point. I was numb everywhere. She laid aside her life to take care of me. Once she found out about her condition, she began to say that she was going to be the sacrifice to bring healing to our family. We were all such a close-knit family, but life's circumstances and differences had driven us apart. She shared things with me about the family, so I could have a better understanding of how to pray for the iniquities of our family. I felt her pass a mantle on to me to help keep the family together.

At this point in my life, it was nothing but the Word of God sustaining me. The hours I spent resting, healing, and eating God's Word sustained me for all the fires I would encounter back to back. I had to declare and decree the promises of God. *I want to emphasize that you need to study, eat the Word, declare, and decree it so you can stand in the day of adversity. Repent for the things you've done that wasn't right, stand still and wait for God to give you instructions and be obedient from that point.* I must say this, we will still have consequences for our actions of disobedience, but the Word gives us understanding of what they are and how to deal with them.

There will be times you will feel like you can't bear the trials, but God promises to help you through it. On Sunday, June 11, 2014, I was in church service and someone beckoned for me to go to the back of church. My mother was standing at the back door. The first thought that came to me was something was wrong with my father. As I approached her, she told me my nephew had gotten shot and pronounced dead. She fell in my arms and cried. It took me a second to process what she said. Surely, she was mistaken and had gotten the wrong information. I took her home and went to the site where the incident happened. My entire family was there with agony written all over their faces. I couldn't imagine how my sister felt to lose her son to such a tragedy. My daughter was on her way to have breakfast with him, they were going to celebrate his birthday, which was the next day. I could not even imagine how my nieces and nephew felt because they were all so close. He was the first male offspring in our immediate family and held a special place in my father's and mother's heart. My mother had come to depend on him to help her with my father. How quickly life is taken. The pain was so great for my family and I felt like there wasn't anything I could do to ease the pain. The only thing I could do was to ask God to comfort my family. With all the Word I had inside of me, at that very moment, I felt hopeless. My heart was hurting. This is something you read about in the newspaper or see on television, yet when it hits home, it is very difficult. It seemed so surreal.

As time progressed we began to heal little by little. He will never be forgotten, but the pain is not as harsh as it was initially. I was at my real testing point. I had to wait on God to heal my body and my heart. We all have a period of waiting to be healed. The perfect timing of God means everything; don't move too soon. **Psalm 27:14** says, *"Wait on the Lord; be of good courage, and he shall strengthen thine heart; wait, I say on the Lord."*

Again, I say timing is everything. You must look back at the promises He made to you. What did He speak to you concerning your future, whether it was through the Word or a prophecy? **Acts 1:4b** says, *"but wait for the promise of the Father which, saith he, ye have heard of me."* God is putting an anointing upon your life. He is endowing you with power. power to press through, power to possess the promise. We don't get the pleasure of knowing His exact timing, but He wants us to trust Him. He is testing you to see if you will remain faithful. What will you do while waiting? Your flesh will react to waiting. It hates waiting. It wants action.

Dr. Mike Murdock says this in his book, called "The Assignment": ***"Waiting also provides God time to address the problems we encounter as Christians in life – miraculously. God is a miracle God. But when you get ahead of Him, you rob Him of an opportunity to prove His power in your life. So, learn to wait."***

1 Peter 5:10 says: *"But the God of all grace, who hath called us unto his eternal glory by Christ Jesus, after ye have suffered a while, make you perfect, stablish, strengthen, settle you."* Waiting on God's timing will produce the desired results of your assignment.

> Joseph waited 13 years
> Abraham waited 25 years
> Jesus waited 30 years.

The Holy Spirit also endows us with the power to wait. They waited in the upper room for the promise of the Holy Spirit which endowed them with **POWER.**

When the bread is taken out of the oven before it is time, it seizes and is not good. Just like us, if we come out of the furnace too soon, we will not be able to be used the way God wants to use us. **Isaiah 25:9** says, *"And it shall be said in that day, Lo, this is our God; we have waited for him, and he will save us; this is the Lord; we have waited for him, we will be glad and rejoice in his salvation."*

It is now time for the bread to exit the fire and cool down. This is the part of the process where we will get our orders from God; we have been fully baked, and it is promotion time. We must wait for the assignment from God. We must remain humble, grateful, and obedient. **Job 23:10** says, *"But he knoweth the way that I take: when he had tried me, I shall come forth as gold."*

The last part of the process of bread is to serve it. Once we have come through the fire, we are fully ready for God to use us to help His people. **2 Timothy 2:21** says, *"If a man therefore purge himself from these, he shall be a vessel unto honour, sanctified, and meet for the master's use, and prepared unto every good work."* Jesus says this in **Luke 22:32**, *"But I have prayed for thee, that thy faith fail not: and when thou art converted, strengthen thy brethren."*

YOU WERE CHOSEN AND MADE IN THE FURNACE OF AFFLICTIONS!

THE REFINER'S FIRE
"You provide the fire and I'll provide the sacrifice"

𝓜alachi 3:3: "And he shall sit as a refiner and purifier of silver: and he shall purify the sons of Levi, and purge them as gold and silver, that they may offer unto the Lord an offspring in righteousness."

The definition of **REFINE** is: (a) remove impurities or unwanted elements from a substance typically as part of an industrial process; (b) improve by making small changes, in particular, make more subtle and accurate.

A refiner's fire is used to refine and purify. It melts down silver and gold, separates the impurities that ruins its' value, burns them up, and leaves the silver and gold intact in a pure state.

Why do we need to be refined? **Psalm 51:5** says, *"Behold, I was shapen in iniquity, and in sin did my mother conceive me."* **The furnace of afflictions in the family of God is always for refinement, never destruction.** If you look at a refinery, it requires intense heat to burn away the impurities to set free the pure metal. The fire is so hot it burns up anything that comes near it

God will sit as a refiner and burn up all our sins to make us pure. No impurity, no sin, no wrong can survive in the presence of God. When God's fire burns, it comes as a consuming fire and burns away everything in us that does not reflect His character. The fire comes to burn away impurities, in order that we will be able to offer sacrifices from a pure heart.

It states in **Deuteronomy 4:24**, *"For the Lord thy God is a consuming fire, even a jealous God."* God's holiness is the reason for His being a consuming fire, and it (holiness) burns up anything unholy. The holiness of God is that part of His nature that separates Him from sinful man. Isaiah asks us "Who of us can dwell with the consuming fire? Who of us can dwell with everlasting burning?" Isaiah says only the righteous can withstand the consuming fire of God's wrath against sin. Sin is an offense to God's holiness. Isaiah also assures us that no amount of our own righteousness is sufficient. **Isaiah 64:6-8** says, *"But we are all as an unclean thing, and all of our righteousness are as filthy rags; and we all do fade as a leaf; and our iniquities, like the wind, have taken us away. And there is none that calleth upon thy name, that stirreth up himself to take hold of thee: for thou hast hid thy face from us, and hast consumed us, because of our iniquities. But now, O LORD, thou art our father; we are the clay, and thou our potter; and we all are the work of thy hand."*

We are tested because God loves us. A father will discipline a child because he loves him and wants to correct the child's wrong actions in order, to protect him from future harm. The heat of God's refining fire comes upon us to burn away those things not like Him and cleanses us from unrighteousness. The fire is also used to train us. It teaches you how to become disciplined in your prayer life. It teaches you to become consistent in the reading of the Word. It teaches you to become more attentive to the voice of God and hear His very heart beat. It teaches you not to be anxious before doing anything. It trains you to hear His voice clearly, and not listen to the voices of men. Man will always have an opinion of what you are going through and what your next step should be. He watches to see if the fire is too hot. He watches to see if you will compromise, take a short cut, or try to manipulate the circumstances so that you do not suffer too long. **NEWS FLASH - if you don't pass the test, you will take it over again.**

When we experience the fires, the trials, and the tests, it really is not a time to complain and murmur. It's a time of getting clarity, understanding and realization that God is working on you. He is making you a new vessel. He is molding and transforming you into His image and His likeness.

Daniel 1:1-8 talks about how king Jehoiakim and the house of Judah was seized by king Nebuchadnezzar of Babylon. The Lord allowed the house of Judah to be taken into captivity. This is a perfect example for those who always try to blame the trials they go through on the enemy. In this passage, we see the Lord gave the house of Judah into the hands of the enemy. It also said that king Nebuchadnezzar asked that certain men of skill, wisdom, cunning knowledge, understanding science and ability be taken from the house of Judah, who they might teach the learning and the tongue of the Chaldeans. They were chosen and was given the kings meat and drink. The king wanted to teach and feed them for three years. They took four vessels from the children of Judah; Daniel, Hananiah, Mishael, and Azariah. The king wanted their names changed to Belteshazzar, Shadrach, Meshach, and Abednego. In a previous chapter, I stated the meaning of their names after they were changed.

We must acknowledge the fact that God gave the house of Judah into the hands of the enemy. They were removed from their place of praise. The enemy wants to separate you from your place of praise. He knows if he separates you from your place of praise, he can steal your joy. If he zaps your joy, he knows that you will be in a hard and dry place. **Psalm 22:3** says, *"But thou art holy, O thou that inhabitest the praise of Israel."* He shows up when you praise Him. Time, and time again you may have been in a dry place, but when you press your way to praise the Lord of Lords and the King of Kings, your situation, or the outlook of the situation changes and it makes way for God to show up and move on your behalf. Your praise is an indication that you have had an encounter with God.

The next thing king Nebuchadnezzar asked was to find a few skillful men, filled with wisdom and ability so that they will be trained and groomed for three years. The enemy is not running after those who are not doing anything, he wants those favored of God, skilled, full of wisdom and has great abilities. Stop trying to figure out why others are not going through what you are going through. You are favored and skilled by God. He will protect and aide you. These are the ones the enemy is seeking to destroy.

The king wanted to feed them his food and give them his wine to drink. He was grooming them for his kingdom work. This is a perfect example of what the enemy wants to do with you. We cannot let the enemy re-define us. We cannot let the world influence us to eat and drink things of the world. We cannot have an appetite and a diet of the world (profanity, pornography, gluttony, greed, alcohol, drugs, demonic video games, etc.). As Christians, we should be influencing the world and not vice versa.

Daniel purposed in his heart he was not going to defile himself with the king's portion. He found favor with the eunuch over them and requested that they be allowed to eat pulse and water for ten days. **Proverbs 3:4** states, *"So shalt thou find favour and good understanding in the sight of God and man."* The eunuch granted favor to Daniel, Shadrach, Meshach, and Abednego and allowed them to partake of their food. **Daniel 1:7** says, *"As for these four children, God gave them knowledge and skill in all learning and wisdom: and Daniel had understanding in all visions and dreams."* Once the 10 days were up, Daniel, Shadrach, Meschach, and Abednego were fairer and fatter in flesh than all of those who ate the kings' meat.

The king communicated with them and found them to have more wisdom and understanding than all the magicians, astrologers, and the men of his kingdom. Immediately after such a great meeting with the king they were tested. King Nebuchadnezzar wanted them to bow down to the golden idol he created. He ordered Shadrach, Meshach, and Abednego to bow down before his golden idol or they would be thrown into a furnace. He gave them two opportunities to bow before the idol and they chose not to defy their God by bowing to another god. Each time they refused to bow. King Nebuchadnezzar had them thrown into a furnace for not bowing down to his idol. Even though they were faithful to the Lord, God allowed them to be thrown into the furnace which was turned up seven times hotter. God allowed this to bring glory to Himself through their willingness to die while having faith in Him.

They had unshakeable faith. The enemy wants us to worship idol gods (cars, houses, material possessions, people, etc.). We cannot compromise, but serve the only one, true and living God. We must stand in faith and not in fear. I know it seems impossible, but God works best in impossible situations. Stretch out on God and in faith, even when you can't trace Him, you must trust Him.

The enemy threw them in the fire, which lets me know that the enemy has a fire and the Lord has a fire. If I had to choose, I would choose to go in the Lord's fire because it comes to make me a new vessel, while the enemy's fire comes to destroy me. The Lord's fire also has the protective covering of the Lord Himself right there with you. Shadrach, Meshach, and Abednego believed that their God was able to deliver them, but if He didn't He was still God and they would not worship another god.

They chose CHARACTER over COMFORT. They did not waver in their faith, they did not bow down to the idols and the demands the enemy had placed on them. They could have bowed down and worshipped the golden image and the enemy would have left them alone, but they chose to have the demeanor that Christ had when He went to the cross.

They chose DISCIPLINE over DISORDER. They refused to bow down to the golden idols of the world. Most of our failures can be traced to an absence of discipline. We fail to keep consistent prayer lives. We fail to speak positive affirmations. We need to control our tongues. We need to have positive confessions and positive declarations. More people are run down by gossip and negative confessions than by automobiles. Gossip kills friendships, disrupts families, divides a church, and assassinates character. Positive confession says you believe God can and will come through. Positive words bring life to dead situations. This is where you must speak those things that be not as though they were.

The three Hebrew boys said with courage in **Daniel 3:17**, *"If it be so, our God whom we serve is able to deliver us from the burning fiery furnace, and he will deliver us out of thine hand, O King."* They positively spoke their deliverance from the enemy.

They chose LOVE over LIFE. Their first love was to God and they did not waver in that love. They knew they could not compromise. They put their love for God over their life. **Matt. 16:25** says, *"For whoever will save his life shall lose it, and whosoever will lose his life for my sake shall find it."*

- Is your love for Christ more important to you than your ambitions or idols?
- Is God more important to you than the pursuit of power or possessions?

- Is God more important to you than the acceptance of worldly desires or your peers?

We are just like Shadrach, Meshach, and Abednego; we are not isolated from painful experiences. There will be times you and I will not escape the trials and tests of life, but if we trust in the Lord, He will bring us through these experiences unharmed and changed.

If you are in a place right now, where you are experiencing the tests and trials that is trying your faith, then you are likely under God's refining fire. The fire is designed to kill all the works of the flesh. **Galatians 5:19** says, *"Now the works of the flesh are manifest, which are these; Adultery, fornication, uncleanness, lasciviousness, idolatry, witchcraft, hatred, variance, emulations, wrath, strife, seditions, heresies, envyings, murders, drunkenness, revellings, and such like of which I tell you before, as I have also told you in times past, that they which do such things shall not inherit the kingdom of God."* If you are living in sin, He will turn away from you, to allow you to realize that you can't survive apart from Him. If you try to live without the Lord in your life, then your own sins will cause you separation from God and cause great pain.

We are living in a time when it is extremely easy to compromise our integrity. We at times, become men pleasers and not God pleasers. The Scripture referenced earlier states that God is a jealous God. For some people, it is easy to compromise their virtue, especially when this type of behavior has become the accepted normality. This kind of compromise will cost you your joy and it will hinder your fellowship with God. It is like the potter and the clay, when we are on the potter's wheel and we are not becoming the vessel He wants us to be, so He smashes us and begins again.

Let us look at the process of the potter and the clay. The meaning of the word **"potter"** in the Old Testament is **"yatsar"**, the one who forms. As we look at the potter and the clay, let's look at the book of Jeremiah. God sent Jeremiah to the potter's house to teach him a lesson.

Jeremiah 18:1-6 says, *"The word which came to Jeremiah from the Lord, saying, Arise, and go down to the potter's house, and there I will cause thee to hear my words. Then I went down to the potter's house, and behold, he wrought a work on the wheels. And the vessels that he made of clay was marred in the hand of the potter: so, he made it again another vessel, as seemed good to the potter to make it. Then the word of the Lord came to me saying, O house of Israel, cannot I do with you as this potter? saith the Lord. Behold, as the clay is in the potter's hand, so are ye in mine hand, O house of Israel."*

God was demonstrating His sovereignty, and this is also how the potter is depicted in the Bible. God is pictured forming man from the earth as the potter forms his clay. **Job 10:8-9** says, *"Thine hands have made me -- and fashioned me together round about; yet thou dost destroy me. Remember; I beseech thee; that thou hast made me as clay; and wilt thou bring me into dust again?"*

Isaiah learned that God was the potter in **Isaiah 64:8** when he states, *"But now O Lord, thou art our Father, we are the clay, and thou our potter, and we all are the work of thy hand."*

As the potter sits at his wheel, turning it, he is concerned for the shaping and the quality of his vessel. With his hands, he adds water to the clay making it pliable. The water represents the Word of God. This makes the clay pliable, so he can mold it and shape it into the image fit for the Masters' use. If the water is not added to the clay, it will become too hard and it will not be pliable enough to create a vessel.

Without the Word, our lives are resistant to the hands of God. Just like the clay, without the water, so are our lives without the Word.

Just as our bodies need water to live and survive, our souls need God's Word to feed us, so our spirit man can grow. **Ephesians 5:26-27** states, *"That he might sanctify and cleanse us with the washing of water by the word,* *that He might present it to Himself a glorious church, not having spot or wrinkle or any such thing, but that it should be holy and without blemish."* God cannot begin to mold and transform us unless we are willing to do our part, study and read the Word of God. If you do not spend time in the Word, then God has little to work with. Just as the potter can't use the clay unless there is water, in the same way God cannot help our process until we get His Word in us.

Let's take a moment to look at the process of the potter and the clay so that we may understand fully the process and the significance of the furnace.

- The clay should be positioned in the center of the wheel. If the clay is not in the center of the wheel it could tear apart before it is finished being shaped. The same way the clay needs to be centered on the wheel, it is the same way a Christian's life should be centered in Jesus Christ before he can mold and shape us. You should be in complete surrender, of your will and your life, letting Him be in full control. If we try to live our lives without the guidance and leading of the Holy Spirit, our lives would fall apart, and we will never reach our divine destiny. **Psalm 31:14-15a** says, *"But as for me, I trust in You, O Lord, You, are my God. My times are in your hands."*

- The potter begins forming the clay by smashing his hands into the center, pushing it down to create an opening. Once this is done, he pushes his hand deep inside the middle of the clay to form it and begins to use his hand to shape it. This is the same way God's own hand is literally going deep into the middle of our souls and spirits where the actual work is done to mold and transform us into the vessels He wants us to be. This part of the process is painful and unpleasant. He is removing negative qualities that He does not want us to have, such as, bad tempers and personalities, pride, jealousy, anger, bitterness, low self-esteem, lust, and immaturity. He begins to shape us to have character, instilling and imparting qualities that He wants us to have. God wants to do inner surgery through the Work of the Holy Spirit.

- As the potter is forming the clay, he is continually applying water to keep the clay from getting too dry and hard. He will keep applying the water as he shapes the vessel. As we continue to apply the Word to our lives, God will continue to shape us and mold us until the vessel takes form. **Ephesians 5:27** says, *"that He might sanctify and cleanse it with the washing of the water by the Word, that He might present it to Himself a glorious church, not having spot or wrinkle or any such thing, but that it should be holy and without blemish."*

- The potter turns the potters wheel "slow" and "steady" to get all the lumps out of the clay. If he turns the wheel too fast, the lump of clay could tear completely apart before it is finished. In the same manner, we must have patience with the Lord on how He wants to work and build our lives up in Him. He usually works things out in a much slower time than we are used to. He knows what you were created to be in this life. A good potter takes his time to create a special vessel. **Psalm 27:14** tells us, *"Wait on the Lord: be of good courage, and he shall strengthen thine heart: wait, I say, on the Lord."*

- Once the clay has been formed, a sharp wire is used to cut the vessel from the potters' wheel. The vessel is then placed on a shelf to dry and harden. The vessel has been shaped and molded by the potter. **Psalm 127:1** says, *"Unless the Lord buildeth the house, they labor in vain who build it."* There will be a cutting away.

- After the clay is dried hard, it is time for it to go into the first firing. It is placed in the fire (kiln) with many other objects that also need to be fired. The vessel can not be affected by the other vessels at this point because once it is hardened, it is set. The fire will increase the strength of the pottery and makes it a permanent vessel.

- Once it is finished the first firing, it is painted a color. This is significant of you coming into the spiritual gifts and call on your life. Specific design, uniqueness and personal markings are put on you.

- After the color has been applied, the vessel then goes through a second firing. Each firing is hotter is hotter and hotter. This firing will permanently embed the design and color in the vessel. When the vessel is placed in the fire this time, it can only go in with other vessels of like color. As you compare yourself to this vessel, this is the time when you begin to flow with those of like callings to grow in your gifts.

- The next step is to glaze the vessel once it comes out of the fire. This process serves as protection, seals to prevent any liquid or substance from penetrating the vessel. This makes the vessel tougher, causes it to shine, and the potter can see his reflection in the vessel. This is likened to the Holy Spirit sealing us and placing an anointing upon our lives. **Isaiah 42:1** says, *"Behold, my Servant, whom I uphold, mine elect, in whom my soul delighteth; I have put my spirit upon him; he shall bring forth judgement to the Gentiles."*

- It is time to go into the fire again. This time the vessel cannot go in the fire with any other vessels. This time it goes into the fire alone. You are being set apart for the work God has created you to do. **Ephesians 2:10:** *"For we are his workmanship, created in Christ Jesus unto good works, which God hath before ordained that we should walk in them."*

- This next step is optional. It is the layer of gold that could be added to give your vessel added value. This is determined by if you are willing to endure another firing. **Job 23:10** said, *"But he knows the way that I take; When He has tried me, I shall come forth as pure gold."*

- The final stage is to go back into the fire. This firing is the hottest firing of them all. No other vessels can go in the fire with you. The fire burns off the impurities from the gold and permanently embeds the gold into the vessel. The brilliance of the gold comes forth, unmistakable for all to see.

Just as the potter sees his image in the completed vessel, our heavenly Father is allowing us to go through our furnace experiences so that we will be in His image and likeness.

Chapter Six

THE PROMOTION IS INEVITABLE
"The furnace in your life is only setting you up for promotion"
(Ranata Barrier)

$\mathcal{T}$he first thing I would like to say is, he (Satan) meant it for your bad, but God meant it for your good. Some of you are in the greatest fire you've ever been in before. Someone reading this has lost their song. The pressures of life, the pressures of family problems, sickness, or being falsely accused has snatched the song out of your heart. Right now, you may be going through some unexplainable situations in your life.

We see marriages of 20, 30 and 40 years ending in divorce. Many of you have lost loved ones to murder, sickness or disease. You have lost homes to floods, tornadoes, fires and/or foreclosure. Vehicles have been lost due to accidents, floods, theft, or repossession. Many have lost jobs due to businesses closing, someone being promoted over you, or you've gotten fired. Maybe your child or children have been lost to the streets, some turning to the ways of the streets after you raised them in the church. Some even believing the street life is better than a Godly lifestyle. Our sons and daughters are vulnerable to things we never thought they would get involved in, putting themselves in positions to be killed and strayed from the truth. They wind up in the wrong place at the wrong time, hit by stray bullets, or become an intended target, and yet, some being innocently killed.

You may have an illness in your body or one of your loved ones. It could be because you don't know God and His healing power. It could be that your faith is weak, or you could be that person who refuses to be taken out by a spirit of infirmity.

Maybe you feel like you are disconnected from God because you have not seen His hand move in a while. You might feel like you are not worthy, or you've messed up too much for God to work in your life. You say you don't hear God speaking anymore. You ask God is He still speaking. You may have developed a "whatever mentality" instead of standing on God's Word. You have experienced cuts, hurts, bruises, embarrassment, picked up doubt, unbelief and, in some cases, you operate in disobedience in the things God has told you to do because of your lack of faith. You are not feeding your faith because you are not reading your Word. You are angry with God because you did not understand why you had to go through the fires you have been through. You have unknowingly hidden bitterness, anger, rebellion, control, retaliation, and rejection in your heart. You say you don't worry, but you're in denial. You are nervous, anxious, overly sensitive, sometimes not sensitive at all, indecisive, impatient, confused, and afraid to step out and believe. You second guess when God tells you to take a risk. You are prideful, insecure, depressed, and withdrawn. You woke up one morning and realized it has been a while since you've caught yourself acknowledging God, not able to pray to the Father or read His Word.

We have had prophecies that still have not yet been fulfilled. It seems that as soon as we get a powerful prophecy, we began to go through the fire. The Word says in **Psalm 18:30**, *"As for God, his way is perfect; the word of the Lord is tried; he is a buckler to all those who trust in him."* In **II Samuel 22:31** you will find the precise same wording of the Scripture.

You must admit you are in the fire. You need to wake up and recognize what God is doing in your life. He has been burning up all doubt, fear, unbelief, rejection, depression and all those things which are keeping you bound. God was right there all along helping you. However, you will stay in that place until you receive deliverance from God. The Lord wants to make sure that your trust is in Him.

You must have confidence in knowing and believing God will never leave you or forsake you. **Keep moving forward despite what you're going through. KNOW this is not your end. Keep working, keep pressing, keep praying.** Joseph kept working even in prison while he waited. He had favor with God and man. He was ruler over the prison and managed it very well. If you find yourself in a bound state right now, just look and see the favor and goodness of God at work in your life. Through all the hell, the tests, the trials, the fires, it's all under the divine providence of God. The definition of **"PROVIDENCE"** is: (1) God is providing protective or spiritual care; (2) timely preparation for future events. It literally means to "see beforehand". Providence teaches that God sees the end or the purpose for what happens in life. He sees and ordains the final goal...so God is actively moving you toward your goal.

Job understood this as he said, *"O that thou wouldest hide me in the grave, that thou wouldest keep me secret, until thy wrath be past, that thou wouldest appoint me a set time, and remember me"* **(Job 14:13).**

When the difficult circumstances show up, many people are quick to say, "God has nothing to do with it", or they say, "The devil is responsible for this." God is God and He is not powerless. Nothing gets past Him; He will allow it, He is always working. What we need to understand is that holding on to God does not mean you won't feel the pain of life. I am sure there will be many nights when you ask, "Why Lord?" or "God what have I done to deserve this?" Believing in God's divine providence doesn't mean you will understand what God is doing; it only means you will trust that God is doing something. The Word says in **Romans 8:28**, *"And we know that all things work together for good to them that love God, to them who are the called according to His purpose."*

God's definition of good is not at all like our definition of good. To us good means it makes us happy or brings us enjoyment. We see good as the absence of pain. God defines good as that which leads to being Christlike or that which brings us to trust Him more.

You are probably wondering if God has forgotten you. He has not forgotten you. He knows where you are, and He knows where you are going. He is getting you into position, so you can accomplish His good purpose for your life. It is not an accident what you are going through right now. There are no accidents in the life of a believer. God has allowed all these circumstances, even the painful ones, because He intends to use every pain for the good; for your good. Without the cross, there could be no salvation, forgiveness, or resurrection. Even in the most terrible situation in life, God is at work in your life; the little things and the big things. The Word says, and we know that it is working for our good.

Are you in a difficult time right now? Do you want to walk away or quit? It may be that God is allowing you to go through this to bring you to this point. He wants you to take a step of faith. Be still and know He is God **(Psalm 46:10)** and He is a rewarder of those that diligently seek Him **(Heb. 11:6)**. He wants you to call upon Him for strength; to look beyond your situation and trust Him in the painful times. Remember this, God is in control and will make all things new.

Every time I went through a fire, I would remind myself that God is allowing this. If He wanted it to stop, He would have brought it to an end. I began to seek God to see what I needed to learn in this furnace, what fruit was I getting pruned, or what fruit was being produced. I learned how to get a worship song to carry me through the season. I had to hold on to the promises from the Word of God and the prophecy I received. I tried not to focus on what someone else was doing or their faults, reminding myself that I needed something from God; I needed to keep my heart right. I should not judge, because I didn't know that person's story or why they were going through what they were dealing with. I finally learned how to get quiet and not run and tell everyone what I was really dealing with, knowing that only God could fix the problem. I constantly asked the Father to keep my heart right towards Him and others. I understood and quoted **John 15:7**, *"If you abide in me, and my words abide in you, ye shall ask what ye will, and it shall be done unto you."*

I did not have a physical husband to depend on. When I encountered any kind of trials, it was just God and myself. I know that He is better than any natural husband. He is a great friend, a great provider, my comforter, my peace when I lay my head on my pillow. He may not have given me everything I wanted, but He sure has given me everything I needed. He has been my protector, counselor, keeper, and friend. For the last 14 years I have been single and kept. If you look at my life when I was younger who knew God could have done this for me. None of it came easy. There were many fires, many tests, and so much pain. **"BUT GOD"** was right there for me. **PAIN** turned into **PROGRESS**.

I want you to notice something in the account of **Daniel 3:20-22** with Shadrach, Meshach, and Abednego. When they were about to be thrown into the fire, the mighty men who were in the army was told to bind them up, put on their coats, their hosen, their hats, and other garments and to cast them into the fiery furnace that was turned up seven times hotter than normal. They were tossed into the furnace being weighed down with all those garments. This depicts how the enemy tries to weigh us down with multitudes of weights to make us lose our focus. Here they are weighed down and being thrown into the furnace. But the Scripture goes on to say that the mighty men of the army burned up when they were putting Shadrach, Meshach, and Abednego into the fire. They burned up at the door. It was a miracle that Shadrach, Meshach, and Abednego had made it thus far.

It is also a miracle you've made it this far. Some of you should have died by now. Some of you should not have made it out of that car accident, survived cancer in your body, kidney failure, a brain aneurism, drug overdose, a divorce that left you for dead, flooding that left you with nothing, a gunshot wound that almost took your life, or losing your loved one you said you could never live without. You should have gone to prison, yes you did the crime, but He kept you from serving the time. God has been merciful to you. There are some people who have gone through a lot less than you and have lost their minds. Right now, where you are, you should be praising God that **you made it to the fire**, because others have died at the door of the furnace. You are *CHOSEN*.

Nobody expected you to make it, but here you are alive, in your right mind, serving God and filled with the Holy Spirit. So, don't complain because you're in the fire. He was with you before you ever got in the fire, and He is not going to leave you now. If you are in the fire, its proof you are coming out simply because you **did not die at the door.**

I just came to tell you he meant it for bad, but God meant it for your good. I know you are saying in your mind, "I really don't know, and I don't understand." Oh! Yes, I do know. I want you to know you are going to make it; you are not going to burn up in the fire. You are coming out because you are being made in the furnace.

Look, when Shadrach, Meshach, and Abednego fell down in the fire, the fire burned up everything that had them bound. When the king looked in, there were four men walking around loose in the fire. Their praise and worship loosened the bands that were holding them bound. I found out when I was in the fire, there were some things in my life I did not need, they were holding me back and it took the fire to set me free. There was some stuff I did not want to let go of; also, some things that did not want to let go of me, and it took the fire to make me loose it. The fire burned up all the weights holding me down.

When you come out of the fire you're going to be loosed and freed from those things keeping you bound. You are coming out healed, you are coming out delivered, and you are coming out with joy, peace, and prosperity. Not just financial prosperity, but spiritual, emotional, and physical prosperity. You are coming out with a greater anointing.

I can hear some of you saying, "But this is a big test, greater than I've ever seen before." **The devil's greatest fear is that you will find out your true purpose and walk in it**. If he has to, he will pull out all the tricks, and try to get his strongest demons to stop you. This means you are a threat to his kingdom and you're getting even closer to your destiny and purpose.

Remember, the first thing the soldiers did was bind them. The devil is always trying to bind our minds, limit us, make us think our hands are tied, trying to make us believe there is no way out. Notice the enemy fully clothed them with garments, hats, coats, and other garments. The enemy wants to weigh us down, so we can't pray, praise and worship. Then he turns up the heat seven times hotter. When the attack becomes greater, the fight gets harder and the enemy becomes more aggressive; it seems like it will never end. The enemy meant it for your bad, but God meant it for your good.

Sometimes we fall, but we must get back up. Don't let the enemy condemn you when you fall to where it seems you cannot get back up. Repent, Repent, Repent from your heart. Mean it and keep moving. Don't give God lip service because He says in His Word He looks at the heart. Get up and tell the devil, **"I am still here. You should have killed me while you had the chance. I did not burn at the door. I made it to the fire and because I did, I'm coming out another vessel."** The very thing the devil tried to destroy you with, **"the fire"**, is the very same thing God is going to use to elevate you.

God is getting ready to elevate you. The fire is not designed to kill you, it's designed to make you meet for the Masters' use. **Isaiah 43:2** says, *"When thou passeth through the waters, I will be with thee,* and the rivers, they shall not overflow thee, when thou walkest through the fire thou shalt not be burned neither shall the flame kindle upon thee."

Shadrach, Meshach, and Abednego came out of the furnace when they were called out, loosed from their binds, and then promoted.

You might be asking God when you are coming out of this fire. When it doesn't matter anymore, when you forget you are in the fire. When you praise, and worship God like you are not even in a fire. When you say, **"it is what it is, but I am still going to praise You God. I am still going to worship You like I was never in a fire."** <u>Before you know it, you have been elevated. Before you know it, promotion has come. You do not even think about the fire any longer</u>. You see the hand of God, the glory of God and the increased anointing of God on your life. **Ecclesiastes 7:8** says, *"Better is the end of a thing than the beginning thereof; and the patient in spirit is better than the proud in spirit."*

<u>IT IS PROMOTION TIME</u>. You went through the fire, tests, pressures, and trials. The devil had his time, but now it is your time. The set time is come. **Psalm 102:13** says, *"The set time to favor her, the appointed time has come."* The **promotion is inevitable; certain to happen, unavoidable.**

God is no respecter of persons **(Act 10:34**). What He did for Shadrach, Meshach, and Abednego, He will do for you. Joseph went from the pit to the prison to the palace. He suffered 13 years before he was able to see his promotion, but Joseph had to forgive those who hurt him.

On July 7, 2007, I remember thinking this was going to be a special day because it was 7/7/7 and according to God's numerical order it was divine completion. I was so excited to see what was going to happen on this special day. I went to a women's fellowship and a couple shared in the meeting about their trials and how God kept them, but they had to forgive each other many times over the years, in order, to allow God to heal their marriage. The Holy Spirit prompted me to call my ex-husband and ask him to forgive me for any wrongdoing that I may have done the 14 years we were together. I called him, but he didn't answer. The Holy Spirit told me to call back and leave a detailed message because I needed to be obedient. I knew in order, for me to move forward in my life I had to forgive him from my heart. The reality of it is, he left me. He had an affair and he divorced me. Yet, God told me to forgive him so that He could use me for His glory. It was when I obeyed God, the weights and burdens of the past rolled away.

Job had everything taken from him. His wife wanted him to curse God and die. The enemy used his friends to make it look like he had done something wrong, but God told Job to pray for his friends. Most times we must pray for the people who hurt us. Not any kind of prayer, but one of sincerity and forgiveness. When Job prayed for his friends, God turned his captivity around and he received double of what he had lost.

When Elisha followed Elijah, the sons of the prophets tried to distract him in **II Kings 2:1-7**, but Elisha had a desire and determination to follow Elijah unto the end. His desire and determination allowed him to receive a double portion and he went from a servant to a prophet. You must have a desire and a determination to see the end results.

IT IS PROMOTION TIME. Somebody just got a revelation from reading this chapter and you were enlightened. You now understand what it means to go through the fire. **THE WAIT IS OVER!** Your moment is at hand. Your faith has passed the test. You have proven to God you can handle the promotion. He can now trust you because you have been tried. **Proverbs 18:16** says, *"A man's gift maketh room for him, and bringeth him before great men."* When God elevates you, people of influence will send for you. Pay attention to these words from **Genesis 41:14** concerning Joseph, *"they brought him hastily out of the dungeon; and he shaved himself and changed his raiment and came in unto Pharaoh."*

When God gets ready to promote you, He can do it within one day, one hour, one second. God can bring your promotion suddenly. Man, woman, you are being promoted now. You have suffered a while, but God is promoting you in this season. God is delivering a miracle to your body. He is healing your mind. He is healing your marriage. Your wayward child is returning home. He is blessing you with that home. He is giving you that car. He is blessing you with that business after all the years you have sown into someone else's business. God is giving you divine connections to fulfill your purpose and destiny. He is blessing you with the resources for your ministry. God is cancelling your debt. He is restoring unto you everything that the caterpillar, cankerworm, and palmerworm had stolen. It looked like you weren't going to make it, but you did and now **IT IS PROMOTION TIME.**

Now that you have been through the fire and you've made it out, you don't even smell or look like what you have been through. As, a matter of fact, there is a glow about you. Yes, I know what it is; it is the fire of the Holy Spirit. **The Holy Spirit has filled you with the fire of God. Igniting you to be a fire starter, a fire spreader; endowing you with the power of God.** You are ready to spread the fire of God everywhere you go; impacting those across the nations and across the airways. You will be just like Jeremiah when he said **in Jeremiah 20:9** (NLT), *"But if I say I'll never mention the LORD or speak in his name, his word burns in my heart like a fire. It's like a fire in my bones! I am worn out trying to hold it in! I can't do it!"*

You are **CHOSEN...and made in the Furnace of Afflictions.** You have been through the fire and now you are the vessel God has created you to be.

A ONE OF A KIND VESSEL; A VESSEL OF HONOR, MEET FOR THE MASTER'S USE.

A PROPHETIC WORD

This is a prophetic word God gave to me in the night hours and He said to share it with His people who are moving into their Day of Miracles

"DAY OF MIRACLES"

Miracles that only I can create. Your infinite mind cannot even imagine what I have created. It is beyond your comprehension.

Get ready for the biggest breakthrough that you've ever had. Spiritual, Emotional, Financial, Healing, and Restoration. Put no limits on me for I will bless abundantly. It is not what you deserve, but it's what I promised. I made a covenant with you and I am not a man that I should lie, nor the son of man that I should repent.

There is a mighty work for you to do in my kingdom. My people are waiting. Massive deliverances must take place. The chains of bondage must be broken off their lives and I need you to go and do the work of the Lord.

Continue to seek my face for there will we meet and commune. It is in this place where I will give you instructions and further directions of where to go, what to do, and what to say. I'm sending you into the earth realm as my mouth piece to speak a word in due season to my people.

It will be in your speaking that will set the captives free. I will go before you and prepare the way and the hearts of the people. They will be hungry for the Word of the Lord and it will be a mighty word that shall flow from your mouth. They will learn of the goodness of God. They will come to know me in a more real way.

Do not be surprised for the way you will begin to minister the word, for it will be me that is doing the work. You will begin to minister in song (prophetically) and through many prophetic acts. I will instruct thee and teach thee in the way you should go. Lean not to your understanding but trust me. Go in confidence and know that I have prepared every place in advance before you get there.

New people shall you fellowship with and new places shall you go. A new song shall be in your heart. New doors shall begin to open, ones that I have prepared for you to go into.

Continually, stay in my presence. Come to me, come to me. Let no one and nothing keep you from my presence.

As you go forth and minster the Word of the Lord, complete healing and restoration will take place in your life. I allowed the pain and rejection so that you could help my people. Those who are going through the same kind of pain. Wounds will be healed, and hearts will be mended. Minds will be renewed, and ministries will be birthed.

Go forth into the highways, bi-ways and nations and do the work of the Lord. For what I have for you to do, no one else can do. Now is the time that I have prepared for you to go forth. No longer will there be any delays. Prepare yourself and come forth to the realm that I have called you to. A new place in me, a place you've never been before. A place higher than you could even imagine.

Keep your focus and trust me. The dams have been broken and the rivers of living water shall begin to flow, like never, before. The healing streams, everywhere they flow, they shall begin to bring life. Healing, Healing, Healing.

Everywhere you go you will find favor. Even your enemies will be at peace with you. My hand is upon you and my anointing have I placed upon you. I send you forth to do the work and the will of the Father.

You will begin to go to a new level of praise and worship. There will be a new realm in me that you will begin to reach. A place so sweet, a place so comforting, a place of safety, a place of serenity. It is in this place that I will begin to deposit in you what I have for you. Come to this place, drink, and sup with me. I long for your fellowship and worship. Let the sweet fragrance of praise just fill the place as we meet.

Come unto me, for I will give you rest, come unto me for I will give you peace, come unto me for I will give you joy, come unto me for I will give you revelation. Revelation of who I really am. You will see me in a way that you've never seen me before for I will breathe a newness into you. A refreshing, a breath of new life.

I long for your fellowship, I long for your obedience, I long for your sweet communion.

COME MEET ME AND LET ME TAKE YOU TO ANOTHER PLACE IN ME.

TO CONTACT THE AUTHOR

RANATA M. BARRIER

WEBSITE: www.ranatabarrier.com

EMAIL: ranatabarrier@yahoo.com

FACEBOOK: @ranatabarrier

INSTAGRAM, PERISCOPE, TWITTER: @ranatabarrier

Made in the USA
Coppell, TX
30 March 2020